Miscarriage

Miscarriage

Overcoming the physical
and emotional trauma

Wendy Jones

THORSONS PUBLISHING GROUP

First published 1990

British Library Cataloguing in Publication
Data
Jones, Wendy
  Miscarriage : overcoming the physical
  and emotional trauma.
  1. Women. Miscarriages. Personal
     adjustment
  I. Title
  306.8'8

  ISBN 0-7225-1869-2

*Published by Thorsons Publishers Limited,
Wellingborough, Northamptonshire, NN8
2RQ, England*

Typeset by Burns & Smith Ltd., Derby.

Printed in Great Britain by Woolnough
Bookbinding Limited, Irthlingborough,
Northamptonshire

10 9 8 7 6 5 4 3 2 1

Contents

Foreword

I was really pleased to be asked to write a short foreword for this book.

My role as Secretary of the Miscarriage Association has reinforced the feeling I had when I miscarried that there just isn't enough information readily available for women and their families when they experience this terrible loss.

Many women describe it as the worst thing that has ever happened to them and quite often they feel isolated. They don't know anyone else in the same position.

This book will help dispel these feelings. Every woman should be able to identify with some of the thoughts expressed by the women who have so generously shared the emotions and sensations they felt. This book is in a way a selection of the stories and letters the Miscarriage Association receives every year. I hope it will help you to come to terms with your loss.

Kathryn Ladley
Secretary, Miscarriage Association

Acknowledgements

I have to thank the hundreds of brave women who have told me about losing their babies. My own experience of miscarriage has been helpful but in talking to them I have realized that others have suffered far more than I did.

I would also like to thank Barbara Pickard, Ph.D., Honorary Research Fellow at Leeds University, for her guidance on nutrition; Dr Joe Jordan, Consultant Obstetrician and Gynaecologist at the Queen Elizabeth Hospital, Birmingham, for his advice on the medical content; Mrs Belinda Barnes of Foresight; and, of course, Mrs Kathryn Ladley, Secretary of the Miscarriage Association, who wanted a book on miscarriage – a woman's experience. I hope this will prove to be what she had in mind and that she likes it.

This book could not have been written without the help of my husband and my eight-year-old daughter, Kathryn. I hope she likes it too – when she is old enough to understand.

Introduction

When it happened . . .

JOANNA, blonde, beautiful and affectionate, felt her life was meaningless. She tried to kill herself.

LIZ, married to a stockbroker in well-heeled Surrey, was deeply depressed. Her husband grew impatient. It nearly wrecked their marriage.

CAROLINE, sixteen and living with her boyfriend, was angry. 'My mother thought it was the best thing that could have happened. Even my boyfriend seemed relieved. I was the only one who cried.'

NANCY, in California, paid a hundred dollars for a dress for her baby to be buried in. 'Everyone thought I was mad but I knew I would never have the chance to dress her up again.'

Different women. Same story. They have all lost their babies in pregnancy.

This book looks at woman's experience of miscarriage – the twentieth-century trauma that is still a tragedy, even in these days of easy abortion and liberated, working women.

More than merely investigating the female angle, this book explores the effects on the entire family. Husbands explain why some marriages crack under the strain of repeated miscarriages. They describe the problems of providing sex to order, love when you *have* to, not when you *want* to. For when a wife is desperate for a child, relationships can come under threat.

ANDY was so upset by the toll that miscarriage took on his marriage that he made an irrevocable decision. He went out and had 'the snip' – a vasectomy.

JOHN turned to drink and developed a real alcohol problem.

IAN worried so much that, at the age of 31, he lost all his hair. Doctors blamed stress.

Here, doctors and medical staff explain the problems of coping with such a traumatic experience; why a miscarriage is more than merely cleaning up the mess, why a woman can be left with years of unresolved grief.

Some women say that their doctors were marvellous. One woman said: 'My doctor was great. He held my hand when he told me that a third baby had died in my womb and I was about to miscarry again.'

Other women say that they were disappointed, hurt and angry, that a doctor who was excellent over every other medical problem was 'totally useless' when coping with a miscarriage.

Some say, 'Doctors don't care. They turn you out of hospital and don't even bother to talk to you.'

One said: 'My doctor was a swine.'

Mothers-to-be face a greater danger of miscarriage now than ever before.

CAROL, 25, knows that from bitter experience. Six months' pregnant and radiant with health – 'I never felt better' – she was suddenly taken ill at work. She had continued to work as a building society manager as she felt so well.

'That afternoon, though, I suddenly felt that I was going down with 'flu. I was feverish, hot and cold, shivery . . . thinking I was in for a nasty dose of some 'flu virus, I left the office early.

'I had a fierce headache. I was so hot and restless that I threw my husband out of bed that night. I had severe vomiting.

'When the doctor called, he realized that I was seriously dehydrated. I had been drinking water but couldn't keep it down.

'The doctor told my husband that he felt that the situation was grave. I was admitted to hospital, put on a drip and the baby was monitored.

'At this point I realized that this was going to affect the baby. Until then I had merely been concerned about my own health – about feeling so rotten myself!

'Then they told me that they didn't think the baby was alive. I had contracted food poisoning and it had killed him. After six months the doctors' tests confirmed that it had been listeria.

'Endless tests were done. Even my two cats were taken away for tests, but cleared. We racked our brains to find out whether it was in something I had eaten and could only put it down to some pre-packed, pre-chilled meat which I had reheated.

'It was suggested that I might have picked it up from animals or mud at a farm where we had spent a weekend. This happened just before the UK Government warnings on listeria and the doctors seemed as baffled as I was.

'Now I tell everyone: if you are pregnant, for God's sake take care what you eat. I had to deliver a dead baby through listeria. Don't let it happen to you!'

Death on the menu

The message on the dangers of food poisoning in pregnancy is getting through to many women now. They are concerned – and confused.

KATE, 31, who lost her first pregnancy: 'I took every care. No drinking. No smoking. But I got food poisoning. Doctors refused to come out to me, saying I wouldn't lose the baby. But I did.'

JULIE, 22, eight weeks' pregnant: 'We have always been urged to eat dairy foods because doctors said they were good for us. Now the Government warns us that cheese and eggs are dangerous and could cause miscarriage. What are the facts?'

Women are worried. **Our daily diet could be lethal, containing deadly bacteria known to attack the foetus in the womb.**

— At least, according to the media. Once upon a time, we rarely heard of miscarriage, of the possibility of losing a baby in the early stages of pregnancy. Nowadays, however, dire warnings are rarely out of the headlines and official pronouncements constantly tell us that our food could kill.

In the UK, Government medical officers have blamed soft cheeses for carrying the deadly listeria bacteria. Eggs are castigated for carrying salmonella. Enough to scare the coolest mum-to-be!

But warnings came too late. When it was revealed in June 1989 that 26 babies had died through listeria – and some experts reckoned the figure was much higher involving as many as seventy cases – a political storm broke and the Health Department was accused of keeping quiet about the problem for two years, as scientists had known about listeria since 1987. Women who have tragically lost their babies demand to know: 'Why weren't we warned before?' Now warnings come almost daily. So often that some experts urge restraint.

'If we go on warning women not to eat ordinary foods, they will end up eating nothing at all – and missing out on the foods the baby really needs,' says nutritionist Dr Barbara Pickard. 'All these warnings are worrying women too much. Often the evidence against everyday things is very slim indeed. But if you mention these things to a pregnant woman – who is super-sensitive, anyway, because of her condition – you may do great damage. She needs to be in a calm frame of mind with no stress!'

Infected food is not the only fear. Hardly a week goes by without some high-level scare about the dangers to unborn babies of apparently innocent things around us: the microwave in the kitchen . . . the simple dental X-ray . . . the VDU in the office. In this book we come clean. We sort out the facts from the fiction, tell you what you *can* eat and what you *can't*. More important, we look at the whole trauma of miscarriage and ask why so many women are upset, baffled and angry. In a recent survey, these women accused the medical profession of providing help which was poor, inadequate and even, in some cases, non-existent. Women talk candidly about their own experiences of miscarriage.

We ask two vital questions: (1) What has gone wrong? (2) Where have we let them down?

CHAPTER 1

If day one was a Sunday . . .
when it happened to me

'Could you come back in half an hour?' The girl assistant in the suburban pharmacy took my signature on the pregnancy test form and disappeared with my small glass bottle, its contents looking surprisingly like good whisky. I stood outside the shop and wondered how to kill the next thirty minutes. What did you do while other people ran a scientific test which would decide your whole future, at least the next twenty years?

The shops were only just opening. I had wanted to get there early, having waited 42 days, as requested. I could have done it myself, of course, with a home kit, but had known I would question the result. I had always been hopeless at science at school. I was bound to get it wrong and wouldn't trust the result. So I went to the chemist, in the same way as I had done before the birth of my daughter, two and a half years ago. Now I wandered into the shops to fill that vital half hour, hardly daring to hope for what I most wanted in the world.

For ages now, I had longed for another baby. I had had my daughter and she was fine, with no problems.

Then, suddenly, I didn't seem to be able to conceive. We had endured all the infertility tests: the post-coital examination, where you rush out of bed after sex so that your doctor can examine you there and then to find out what is going wrong! Even a laparoscopy operation where the gynaecologist puts a kind of surgical telescope through an incision in your navel, to find out what is happening. Then, of course, there had been the working out of the calendar dates to make sure we were making love at the right time, that vital middle-of-the-month two days. You might not be in the mood, of course; your poor, long-suffering husband might be exhausted after a business conference . . . it didn't matter. There were nights when you had to – or you would miss the chance for another month. At my age, I hadn't got time to wait. In my late thirties, the biological clock was ticking ominously away.

I had to get another baby in while I still had the opportunity, save my daughter from the hideous fate of being the 'only child'.

How unscrupulous I became, arranging dates, times, studying the calendar.

My desire for another child had become almost an obsession, overriding consideration for other people. A total need. My gynaecologist had said after the laparoscopy: 'There is no reason why not. You are fine and so is your husband.' So we went on 'trying', went on adding up and working out dates: 'If Day One was a Sunday . . . tomorrow is Day Fourteen.' We tried – no one could say we didn't. I had begun to wonder – was it my own fault? I had had a good career, never thought much about children, except as something I would have in the far-away future. Then I'd been lucky, got pregnant, had a child just when I wanted it, with no drastic alterations to my plans.

While pregnant, I had worked abroad, hiccuped happily around Ibiza, toured the art galleries and churches of Venice, taken the ferry to Elba . . . and Kathryn had been safe inside me on all those 'trains and boats and planes'. All was well.

Surely, it was fashionable, wasn't it, to have late babies, after you had done all the other things you wanted to do in life? Didn't all the film actresses do it? Weren't all the newspapers and magazines always full of the obstetric successes of ladies old enough to be grandmothers. Now distractedly, I bought frozen food and wondered: Was it so easy, really? Had the media got it wrong?

Perhaps I had been too lucky. The girl who had everything, according to my local paper's publicity. I thought, guiltily, as I shopped, about all the things I had wanted, more than babies. Maybe, my failure to conceive was some kind of almighty nemesis. Morbidly, I wondered whether I was being punished for being too lucky. I paid for frozen peas and looked at my watch. It was time to pick up the result.

A small mean brown envelope, sealed, was handed to me. I waited until I was outside the shop to open it. My fingers were cold and clumsy. Uncertain sun flickered through to the street which was gathering momentum for the day's business. The message was cool and clinical. It was set out as an Either/Or arrangement. One version said: 'Your pregnancy test was *negative*. You should see your doctor if menstrual irregularities persist.' The other said: 'Your pregnancy test was *positive*. You should see your doctor as soon as possible.' The pharmacist had deleted version one. I was pregnant.

Wow! I must have been forgiven my sins, after all. Divine absolution must have flowed upon me even while I shopped in the Sainsbury's supermarket. I was having a baby! I was so pleased. I told everyone, recklessly, at this early stage. When I collected my daughter from nursery school, I told her teacher. My husband, answering the telephone in his office, said, 'Told you it would be all right, if you were patient!' He brought half a bottle of champagne home from work.

I went to the shops to see all the wonderful new prams. I got out my baby book to look up the pictures of foetal development in the womb. 'In the sixth week, the ears take shape' . . . I pictured my baby getting on with all that while I was driving the car or getting the breakfast. I hoped it would be another girl. Julia Frances, I thought, the Frances being after my mother-in-law. Kathryn had been called Kathryn Eileen after my mother so that was fair.

All the way round Europe, when I had been expecting Kathryn, I had thought the baby was cushioned and secure in her sac of fluid inside me. This baby was safe now. It never occurred to me that anything could go wrong. **No one ever tells you that you could miscarry.**

In the ninth week, I started to bleed. Just a little, but enough to worry me. My gynaecologist said, 'I'm sure it's fine but we may as well do a scan.' The ultrasound scan gives you sound-wave pictures of the baby.

A great moment – to see all those fuzzy outlines and have a radiographer interpret them for you, as they did when I was expecting Kathryn. 'Your baby is moving about.' It had been great news then.

This time the operator didn't say much but she asked me about my dates. The junior doctor said, 'A bit small for dates, but probably all right,' and examined me to make sure the cervix was closed. I went home, not knowing the veiled message of that comment: 'A bit small for dates'. Three weeks later I began to bleed again. This time it went very quiet in the scan room. I lay in the customary uncomfortable position: a gel smeared across my bare and swelling abdomen while the instrument passed across it could pick up the sound-waves and translate them into a blurred image on the screen. I had drunk the required two pints of liquid and was not allowed to pass water, so that my bladder would be swollen and make images clear. In this position, you have no inclination to stop and hold a long discussion.

You want to get it over quickly and head for the Ladies! But the operator was taking her time, struggling, passing the instrument from side to side as she searched painfully for something she couldn't find. Her indrawn breath was sharp and tense. Because I was naive and did not realize that she was not supposed to comment, I pressed her for a verdict. I asked to to tell me what was the matter.

'I can't find a heart-beat,' she finally admitted. The young doctor was summoned. So well intentioned, he groped to communicate with me in my world which was outside his youthful bachelor understanding, his just-out-of-college cocoon. He seemed to think I was worried about my own health.

'Don't worry,' he said. 'We can do a D and C. Quick as a flash!' That is not what I want, actually. His 'D and C quick as a flash' – what he saw as a blur on the hospital screen was my Julia Frances. The scan operator pointed out that she could see the other essential products of conception on the screen.

The developing amniotic sac was clearly visible. But there was no heart-beat.

I was to come back in a week, just to be sure.

At home, I ploughed through medical books, found the crucial definition – *Blighted ovum*: 'This sometimes occurs in pregnancy, when the embryo fails to develop beyond a very basic stage. A blighted ovum always aborts spontaneously.' In medical parlance, that meant miscarriage. Inevitable. Certain. It was a random event, said the books, a hard-luck situation.

'Julia Frances,' I asked in that hopeless

waiting week. 'What happened to you? Did you just die quietly while I was so happy? What was I doing when you died? Buying baby clothes or loading the washing machine?'

The medical people had told me that if I didn't have a miscarriage naturally, they ought to scrape out the uterus with a D and C. An Irish friend, a Catholic, consoled me: 'Don't let them take it away. It might be all right. That machine could have made a mistake.'

I clutched at that illogical hope. I didn't understand technology, was easily baffled by computers.

Perhaps they'd got it wrong and my baby was, even now, catching up with her development. I pictured her sitting up and taking nourishment in my uterus. Confounding the experts, becoming a miracle in six months' time.

After all, I still felt pregnant, was still hiccuping a lot, had great, swollen heavy breasts. My gynaecologist, who was also a good friend, rang me. 'It's the placenta,' he said. 'That's still working and making you feel pregnant.' I imagined my body as an empty nursery. All the equipment – the sac, the placenta, ready for the new baby . . . Only the baby had died and it was all a waste of effort.

Still I hoped. Until I went back for that final scan. There was still no heart-beat. There was the sac, foolish now, ready for a child who would never be. The D and C was booked for me.

But before I went back for the operation, I had the experience suffered by 45 per cent[1] of all pregnant women in the UK every year.

I had a miscarriage.

Miscarriages – just how many are there?

At least 30 per cent of pregnant women experience the loss of a conceived baby before the 28th week (seventh month) of pregnancy. Professor Richard Beard of St Mary's Hospital, London, states: 'This figure may be even higher, for 15 per cent of pregnancies end in a spontaneous abortion (miscarriage) that can be recognized by the woman and her doctor. A further 28 per cent of pregnancies are lost so early that they are clinically unrecognizable, occurring so close to the next period that they are interpreted simply as a late period.'

The empty nursery

Between 30 and 40 per cent of all miscarriages are blighted ovum miscarriages, when the woman's body develops normally and is completely pregnant. The placenta develops to filter the hormones for the baby's nourishment. The amniotic sac (the bag of waters) enlarges, to provide a safe, secure home for the baby for nine months.

The woman has all the normal pregnancy symptoms: enlarged, heavy breasts, swollen with the effects of the hormones, oestrogen and progesterone, which are swimming around in her body. She feels sick sometimes in the mornings. She is tired, lethargic and can't face her food.

Inside her body, the placenta and sac are growing steadily. All the equipment for the baby's needs is ready. A pregnancy test shows a positive result. The nursery is prepared. The proud mother-to-be is counting the months and starting to tell her friends. She has booked her first antenatal appointment and gives her dates happily to the receptionist. She is three months' pregnant.

Then comes the shock. In the scan room, the operator of the ultrasound scan complains that the baby seems 'small for dates'. The silence grows heavy as she tries desperately to find a heart-beat.

Because the one vital ingredient of that nursery is missing. There is no baby.

In blighted ovum cases, the cluster of cells has failed to develop very early on, at some basic stage.

The nursery is empty.

The mother has to be told the awful news. She is certain to lose her baby. If it does not come away as a natural miscarriage, it must be removed by surgery.

No one knows why so many pregnancies end like this. 'All we know is that the first sign is picked up on the scan and we think first of all that the foetus is small for dates,' says Dr Joe Jordan, Consultant Gynaecologist. 'But a further scan, perhaps a week later, may confirm this and we just have to say, "Sorry. No baby."

'As many as two-thirds of all conceptions are lost,' he says, 'and a large percentage of them are blighted ova. In any pregnancy, there is vast wastage of sperm from the male and eggs (ova) from the woman. In this case it is just that an unhealthy sperm or unhealthy egg has been involved in fertilization. A random event. A "hard luck" situation.'

When it happened to me, I couldn't believe it. I had been pregnant before and felt exactly the same. I hoped, illogically, that the hospital technology would be wrong. It was a futile hope. Many women get very upset and angry. They feel that in some way it must be the doctor's fault. But there is nothing he can do to save the pregnancy. Sometimes, there will be early signs that all is not well, perhaps the loss of a little blood or brownish discharge. Too often, there is no warning at all and the verdict from the hospital comes as a complete shock.

Usually, a miscarriage happens naturally and, unless there has been an ultrasound scan, a woman may not know that it was a blighted ovum. Now that hospitals have the technology to detect blighted ova, a D and C is normally done.

LESLEY, a social worker, was unmarried when she became pregnant. Her lover was delighted. They have an ongoing relationship although they do not live together. But Lesley was told that the case was a blighted ovum and that she must lose the pregnancy. 'We both felt cheated. He felt that he had somehow been "conned" – that the pregnancy we had planned for just hadn't been a baby at all. It was difficult to know what to tell people. The hospital staff were very kind.

'They explained that the baby had not developed properly and that I had a choice of letting them take it away or waiting until I lost it naturally, but that would mean a risk of infection. I felt that nature had played a trick on me. But it is easier for me now to know that I don't need to grieve for a developed baby. It would have been harder to lose a proper baby.

'The social worker at the hospital was kind, but she said such things as, "You can try again. You are still young." I knew that. I'm only 34. But she seemed to think I was in a conventional situation. Being unmarried does make a difference. When I was told I had a choice, I felt like saying, "Hold on. Leave me alone and the baby might recover." But I knew that wouldn't happen, so I opted for the D and C.'

ANNE, a policewoman, was told that her baby had met the same fate and disintegrated in the womb. 'I'm normally a steady, sensible kind of person, but I'm ashamed to say I fell apart in front of the scan when they told me. I sobbed hysterically.

'The radiographer only said, "It's a bit small. I shall make my recommendation to your doctor."

'Eventually a houseman came and told me that the baby was dead and they would operate that evening.'

When her pregnancy began, Anne had been busy with a successful career in the police force but, at 26, she also wanted a family. 'The baby was conceived during a long-overdue weekend with my husband. He never has much free time, with his own business to run, so it was quite unusual to get a weekend to ourselves.'

She didn't tell her colleagues that she was expecting a baby. 'Silly pride, I suppose, but I didn't want them to feel that they had to treat me differently. Policemen generally consider pregnant policewomen to be at least a liability, though I've heard comments which were stronger than that! Murphy's Law, I suppose, but the minute I was pregnant I seemed to be sent on assignments which were more dangerous than before.

'I spent one night creeping across a field trying to catch a gang with metal detectors who had beaten up a male colleague the night before.

'I went to check out an unoccupied house and a gun came out of an upstairs window, pointing straight at me. I was sent to chase up a thug who had hijacked a car and forced someone to drive it at gun-point!

'Then I was involved in a training course where fitness played a large part and I had to go on a three-mile run. Mine was more of a trot, I admit!' It was during this course that she noticed some bleeding. 'I was scared, but daren't tell anyone as I had been too proud to tell anyone I was pregnant.' Back home, she spent a day in bed. 'But when I stood up the blood just rushed out. My husband rang the hospital and we waited for the ambulance.

'My husband broke down while we were waiting. He had previously thought about being a father but not about me. Now he was really worried about me. Probably he thought I was going to die.'

After telling her that the baby was dead, the hospital sent her home as they were too busy to operate immediately. 'I had to stay at home that night. I can't tell you how terrible I felt. I'd stopped bleeding. The baby was still there but they were going to take it away.'

Doctors are cautious about diagnosing a blighted ovum. The sac can be seen from Week Six of pregnancy and an embryo from Week Seven[2] when a diagnosis of blighted ovum could be made. To be on the safe side, doctors prefer to wait and only make a diagnosis of 'absence of foetal life' after Week Ten. There is also the possibility that the mother has got her dates wrong and they have to allow for this. The sac in a blighted ovum case is often smaller than in a normal pregnancy. Blighted ovum cases occur in between 30 and 40 per cent of all miscarriages.[3]

Dr H. Robinson, in the *Journal of the Royal College of Obstetricians and Gynaecologists*, warned doctors in 1977: 'A clinical decision to terminate a pregnancy should only be taken once the operator has seen a large number of similar cases and has made the diagnosis without error.'

CHAPTER 2

The victims

'Life is absolute hell. I feel hurt, angry and completely in the dark. If anyone else says, "Never mind, you can have another," or, "It's nature's way of telling you something was wrong with the baby," *I shall scream!*'

'Why didn't any doctor bother to tell me what to *do* when I had a miscarriage? Why did no one warn me I might haemorrhage? How was I to know the dangers?'

'It happened seventeen years ago, but I have never got over it. The depression lasted years and nearly broke up my marriage. All because no one talked to me about it.'

'It was the best thing that could have happened – according to my mother. My boyfriend was relieved. I was the only one who was heartbroken. I'd wanted that baby so much, even though I was only sixteen.'

'I've lost fourteen babies through miscarriage. After losing them, the hospitals just sent me home. "Better luck next time," they said – but it's all such a waste! One of those lives might have been a Prime Minister!'

Miscarriage, modern style. The words of women who have lost their babies early in pregnancy, usually before the fourteenth week. Often miscarriages happen so early that the woman herself doesn't even know she is pregnant and puts it down to a 'late period'.

In this book we investigate the trauma of miscarriage. A cry of anger comes from the women who have experienced it. Members of the Miscarriage Association involved in a recent survey revealed that 80 per cent were left feeling angry and bitter. Of these, 66 per cent thought the medical treatment they received was inadequate, even poor.

These women complain that they received:

no information;
no counselling;
no advice.

Often, after a miscarriage, a woman goes home to relatives who, though well meaning, carefully avoid the subject – *just* at the time when she most needs to talk about it. A woman who weeps for a child lost at three months' gestation receives little sympathy.

'It was only a cluster of cells, a life

hardly started,' is a common attitude, the amount of sympathy apparently measured by the length of time she was carrying the baby.

If it is a still-birth, things are different. A child lost after the 28th week is technically a still-birth, not a miscarriage. Parents receive more consideration. Husbands are often allowed to stay in hospital with their wives. Enlightened hospitals take photographs of the dead infant – pictures which are treasured for life by the parents as a record of the only time they ever saw their child. The only tangible evidence of his life and death.

In still-birth there is also a burial. All the rigmarole of the death ritual to comfort the grieving parents.

In a miscarriage, where a child is lost much earlier, there is usually very little ceremony. The medical remedy is straightforward, usually a D and C (Dilation and Curettage) operation to scrape the womb clean and ensure all its contents have been expelled.

A minor operation, an overnight stay in hospital, perhaps a little speech from a junior doctor. 'No one knows why,' he may explain. 'These things are very common. Better luck next time.'

The products of conception are whisked away out of sight to the hospital sluice and she goes home. Only as little as 24 hours ago she was admitted, an expectant mum still. Now it is all over and she is alone again. To go home with a million questions still in her mind, some of which no one can ever answer.

'Why did it happen?'

'Was it a boy or a girl?'
'Will it mean I can't have other children?'
'How soon can I try again?'

These are the big questions. Understandably the medical experts honestly don't know many of the answers themselves. Nine times out of ten, a doctor does not know *why* a miscarriage happens, and could rarely tell you the sex of the child.

But women are often left without answers to more simple, practical matters: such as the length of time they can expect their bleeding to continue after miscarriage, whether they should use tampons or sanitary towels. 'I'm amazed they are never told these things,' says Heather Robertson of the Miscarriage Association. 'There is a positive danger from infection if they use tampons after miscarriage – but no one *tells* them.

'Some don't even know what operation they are having. A D and C completely clears out all remnants of the pregnancy, but one young woman said she thought it was to help her keep the child.'

After a miscarriage, a woman is told to forget it and get on with her life. **She is never encouraged to discuss it. She is never given permission to grieve.**

That is why so many women now turn to the volunteers of the Miscarriage Association for the counselling and help that professionals have failed to give. In this book, we look at the work of this organization and the practical and emotional support it offers to parents. We also look at medical achievements in research.

The breakthrough

For years, women have endured recurrent miscarriage, with its consequent agonies of despair and sense of failure. Now at last has come the Good News.

Doctors have discovered that, in a vast number of cases, there is a way of actually preventing it. A woman can be immunised against miscarriage. Pioneer of this treatment in the UK is Richard Beard, Professor of Obstetrics and Gynaecology at St Mary's Hospital, Paddington, in London.

Says Professor Beard: 'There is no need for these women to be Cinderellas any more. Let's face it, after suffering a number of miscarriages, a woman is in a dreadful state about it, emotionally. It needn't happen.'

Immunologists have found that many women have an immune system which rejects the foetus as 'foreign' and this is the cause of their miscarriage. But now they can be injected with their husbands' white blood cells. This stops them from rejecting the baby and they can go on to have a successful pregnancy.

'It may not work for everyone,' says Professor Beard. 'But I can give you a *take-home baby rate of 70 per cent.*'

The treatment of immunotherapy is now being used with some success in many centres in the UK, with notable research being carried out in Cambridge. Many mothers get their 'miracle' babies this way.

But while the medical news is good, the fact remains that some women still have to endure miscarriage which, if not handled well at the time, can result in a lifetime's grief.

Miscarriage – the mystery

'What is it really like to have a miscarriage?'

Most women who have never experienced it want to know the answer to that simple question. There is no reason why they should know what it is like – the subject has been a taboo for so long that there is little information easily available. Books on babies and pregnancy normally dismiss miscarriage as 'something that happens in rare cases', as though anxious not to sow even a seed of alarm into the prospective mother's thoughts.

That's fine, for the thousands whose children arrive safely. But for the rest of us – well, it would have been nice to have been prepared!

Miscarriage is in many ways like a dress rehearsal for real labour. A rehearsal for childbirth with all the contractions and none of the cuddles.

I had a miscarriage in McDonalds! At least, it started among the French Fries and the Big Macs – not that it was anything to do with the McDonalds food. The miscarriage had been 'threatening' for days. We were only there to try to encourage my two-and-a-half-year-old daughter to eat, as she much preferred a paper bag to a plate! I scuttled home with her before I became an embarrassment to the restaurant. I drove home fast, my abdomen gripped spasmodically by the strong contractions of giving birth. The labour pains were familiar, the ones which come at the same time as that single moment when you gaze at the delivery room's electric lights above you and know that it is too late, much too late, to change your mind. This is one decision you can't go back on. The life force has taken over so powerfully that, for once in your life, you have no choice.

I felt like that in childbirth and recognized it again now. Having my daughter, Kathryn, had been a totally happy experience. Now, in the throes of miscarriage at thirteen weeks, I felt similar physical sensations. Only the happiness was missing. I had no desire to push this baby out. I wanted the child inside me, safe for another six months.

Fast escape from a fast-food restaurant! It was no place for the drama of miscarriage!

At home, children's television distracted Kathryn's attention. The 'voices' of glove-puppets Sooty and Sweep struck an incongruous note of normality. Four o'clock, tea time – usually the most normal hour of the day. Now only one thing made it different – the ominous pumping of my uterus, the tight pain of contractions. I was not afraid of having a miscarriage. Almost from the start, this pregnancy had not felt 'right'. It had been what the

medics call a 'threatened miscarriage' for ages and I should have been prepared. I had thumbed through the medical books, actually, but found very little information on the subject.

Babies now! They were different. I knew all about babies. Those live bundles in nappies held no fears for me, for hadn't I read all the plentiful literature in women's magazines and all the 'How to Have a Baby' books under the sun?

I knew how to prepare for them, what to buy at Mothercare, how to furnish the nursery, relax in labour, the minute details of psychoprophylaxis . . . even what song to sing to get me through the labour.

'The Grand Old Duke of York,' I would carol, encouraged by my midwife, a devotee of natural childbirth.

As far as it is possible for any mother to be, I had been trained for my first pregnancy. I knew how to give birth. I did not know how to have a miscarriage. I was afraid of my own ignorance and the worst thing was not knowing what to expect. To put it crudely, I did not know what it would look like when it came out or how I would feel.

The nearest I had ever come to miscarriage was to watch it on films where the expectant mum was suddenly taken away in a wheelchair to a waiting ambulance. Even the pub landlady Bet Lynch in the TV Soap opera *Coronation Street* had had that sort of treatment when she was supposed to have lost her baby in the 'Rover's Return' pub. Hushed tones all round, worried faces, high drama . . . the screen faded to black and the credits rolled.

As for the mechanism of miscarriage

– what would actually happen to me – well, frankly, I knew nothing. Absolutely nothing. Only my mother had given me an idea: 'Don't worry about what to expect. It will probably only look like a lump of raw liver.' You needed a strong stomach to discuss the details – just as, perhaps, you needed a strong stomach to discuss any human process, even childbirth.

Only in childbirth, the less lovely details are blurred by emotion. The joy of a baby's safe arrival mists it all into soft focus. But there I was, right in the middle of a miscarriage, my only idea of the experience gained more from MGM than medical knowledge – the heroine falls down the long sweeping staircase, loses the baby and is whisked away to hospital.

But it is not like that in real life and I intend to tell you exactly what it *is* like to have a miscarriage, in case, one day, it happens to you or someone close. When you have read this book you will not be ignorant, as I was. You will know what to expect.

Whose fault is it anyway?

'Was it something I did?'

Afterwards women start to blame themselves. After miscarriage you feel something akin to bereavement. It is only natural that you should start feeling guilty about something you did, in the same way that you find something to feel guilty about when a loved one dies.

What causes a miscarriage?

It is hardly ever something as obvious as a dramatic fall down a flight of stairs. But many of us will immediately blame the heavy load of shopping we carted from Sainsbury's supermarket, the gin and tonic we drank at that party, something we ate or even the X-ray we had at the dentist's.

Guilt about our past will come to the fore. What about that termination in our teens? Could an abortion in our previous history have caused all this

trouble now? The chances are, say doctors, that your miscarriage is nothing whatsoever to do with anything you did. It is far more likely to be caused by your body's reaction to the pregnancy such as the immune reaction researched by Professor Beard, some physical defect in the body which is outside your control, or a defect in the sperm or ovum which make up the baby.

It is known, for instance, that 50 per cent of all miscarriages happen in cases where the foetus is abnormal and would not have been able to survive on its own. The old wives' tale about 'Nature's Way' of sorting out the defective babies may have a lot of truth in it.

These days, when we know so much about the effects of our actions on the developing foetus, it is easy to become paranoid, and to think that everything around us may harm the baby.

One woman told me: 'I spent my

pregnancy in a state of worry. The little girl next door had chicken-pox. I worried in case it would affect my baby, like German measles, which can cause blindness.

'If I had a headache, I daren't take an aspirin. If we went to a party, I daren't risk a drink. I was even afraid that the microwave in the kitchen would harm it.'

In this book, we look at the possibilities. What are the dangers that can cause miscarriage? We shall examine the evidence which links miscarriages with: alcohol; smoking; drugs; X-rays; a previous induced abortion; getting ill in pregnancy or being in contact with childhood illnesses; food poisoning – salmonella or listeria.

There are environmental dangers all around us, for example:

1 *Pollution in the atmosphere.* Miscarriages followed the dioxin explosion at Seveso, Northern Italy and outbreaks of miscarriages have occurred in areas which have been sprayed with chemicals such as 245T, which contains dioxin and which was used in Vietnam as a defoliant.

2 *Hazards in the home and office.* There is also evidence against the VDU (Visual Display Unit) of computers used in most offices these days. Five out of fourteen pregnant women working with VDUs at a BBC newsroom in 1988 had miscarriages. Over a period of eighteen months there have been fourteen miscarriages among 100 women working at the headquarters of *USA Today* in the United States.

A researcher at the US National Institute of Environmental Health Sciences has recommended further investigation of the cluster as it was 'an unusual number'. A recent study of VDUs in California reported that women who used VDUs for longer than half the working week during the first three months of pregnancy were more likely to suffer miscarriages than those doing other types of office work.

In the next chapter we meet the highly motivated women whose work over the past decade has helped many women through the horror of miscarriage.

CHAPTER 3

The helpers

'I saw this girl lying in hospital, alone in a side ward, with a dead baby inside her. She was about to go to theatre. I thought, "No one should be allowed to go through this alone. Especially at eighteen." '

Karen Spencer is speaking. She used to be a nurse. She has had several miscarriages, but it was not until a visit to a hospital some years later that she caught sight of the side-ward patient and knew she had to take action.

'I had thought during my miscarriages that there was a need for more support. After I saw that girl I was certain.'

Karen set up the Miscarriage Association, coping single-handed with the sacks of mail. It soon became obvious that women needed such an organization and newsletters had to be written, meetings organized, telephone counselling provided.

Publicity snowballed rapidly, in the way that self-help organizations become known and catch on. Running it from her home in Bristol, Karen soon found that her own health was not up to the strain. 'I was even writing the newsletter on my own.'

Disabled, anyway, with a heart and

kidney condition, she struggled on until she finally collapsed suffering from nervous exhaustion.

'I had wanted to run it. I knew how much it was needed, but running a self-help organization on your own really is a killer,' says Karen.

At that time (in the early 1980s), a new member had joined who was able to help. Charlotte Gilroy had had two miscarriages. She has now had four. A social worker, from Dewsbury, Yorkshire, she stepped in at the time of Karen's collapse.

'I had been horrified that in this day and age – the day of the self-help organization – there had been nothing to help me over my miscarriage,' says Charlotte. 'I soon found myself talking to women who were suffering exactly the same feelings as I had done. After miscarriage you are trying to cope with three hidden things: hidden loss, hidden grief and hidden reality. You desperately need some evidence of your pregnancy. There is nothing tangible after miscarriage – nothing to hold on to.'

The headquarters of the Miscarriage Association had by now switched to

Yorkshire. There were days when Charlotte hardly left the telephone. 'Calls would go on all day. I would answer the phone in my dressing-gown early in the morning and still be talking to distraught women at four o'clock. One day I was still in my nightie at tea time!

'I was not going out to work, so I was able to give it my full time. Women seemed to have such a great need to talk through the experience. The newsletter's most popular contributions came from members who told their own stories, going through all the detail, the minutiae of the event. The story they needed to tell someone who had the patience to hear it repeated over and over again. There are not many relations, no matter how sympathetic, who are willing to listen patiently to that kind of repetition!' Charlotte herself had found that one of the strangest aspects of losing her own baby was the law on burial. 'I found that I was not allowed to bury the foetus in my own garden. I could bury a dead cat but not a human foetus.

'I got round that by burying it in a plant pot.' When Charlotte retired from her voluntary job as secretary, it was for the happiest of reasons. Two successful pregnancies had brought her a family at last.

The association's next office was a walk-in wardrobe! Heather Priest had no room for an office in her tiny terraced house. So she crammed the telephone, the files, a desk and an angle-poise lamp into a walk-in wardrobe. 'It worked,' she says. 'I dealt with all the calls and letters, all the tragedies of miscarriage, from that little cupboard.'

Heather, who has worked in catering and is now communications officer for a transport authority, remembers 'dealing with a distraught mum on the 'phone in the cupboard while watching Sarah, my toddler, wreck the room.' However, she wanted to do it. Heather and her lorry-driver husband had badly wanted a family but she lost a baby at 25 weeks.

'Another three weeks and it would have been classed as a still-birth and I'd have had all the trimmings. Photographs, a burial, the lot! As it was only 25 weeks, they took the foetus away quickly. I asked what they had done with it and they replied, "You don't want to know that, do you!"

'By the time I had pulled myself together enough to demand to see it, they told me it was too late. I persuaded a nurse to break the rules – I think she risked her job – and she looked up the hospital records for me. It said, "Child lost at dissection. All internal organs intact." That child had weighed one pound and two ounces [510g]. Ironic when you think that a special baby unit can now keep alive a child weighing only one pound [just under half a kilo]!

'I would have liked to have seen him, hold him, at least have him buried, but I had no choice. It took me two years to recover from the grief although my husband was tremendously supportive. He cried too.'

A further pregnancy followed. Her daughter Sarah was born by Caesarean section.

'I blame the fact that I was grieving so long after the miscarriage that I never had a good relationship with Sarah. I had a strange feeling that I was looking after her but that I wasn't really her mother . . . Someone else would soon come along and collect her. As if I were baby sitting.'

Heather feels she never worked through the experience of miscarriage. She is now divorced (nothing to do with losing the baby) and works full time while Sarah is looked after by her grandparents. 'When she was born the porters in the hospital were smashing. They never once wheeled me into the room where I had lost Joseph. I gave him a name at the suggestion of women at the Miscarriage Association. You can't go on talking about anonymous "it" for ever.

'I cried so much after that first miscarriage. Once, out shopping, I saw a baby in a pram and only just managed to stop myself snatching it away. I just wanted to cuddle it. I rushed off to my doctor's instead and said, "Come on, you're more sensible than that!"

'He gave me tranquillizers. It made me understand how people feel.

'The urge to hold a baby is almost overwhelming when you have just lost one.

'Friends who had just had their baby were very doubtful about visiting me. When they eventually did they kept looking at me very warily. I felt like saying, "Don't worry. I'm not going to make off with your baby!"

'It was such a late miscarriage. I was nearly ready for the baby. I had even ordered the nappies. When I went into the shop the salesgirls asked, "What did you have?"

'It helped me a lot to become involved with the Miscarriage Association. The only reason I couldn't carry on with the work was the fact that I needed to work for a living and the organization became so big.'

When Kathryn Ladley came to the association it was already well established as a national charity, with a small office in Wakefield, Yorkshire. A grant from the DHSS means that they can afford proper equipment and to pay part-time clerical staff.

Originally, like her predecessors, Kathryn was seeking help herself. Highly educated, a professional woman who practises as a quantity surveyor, she had found that having a miscarriage had left her stunned, shaken by the silence surrounding the subject.

'People avoided talking to me about it, making it more a conversational taboo than cancer or death. Outsiders often said, "Never mind. You can have another one." People wouldn't dream of being so tactless to someone who had just lost a three-day-old baby. Anyway, after a miscarriage, it's not another one you want. It is *that* one – the child you've just lost.'

Short, dark and determined, Kathryn Ladley was lucky. She went on to have a further pregnancy which was successful in spite of a medical condition which meant she spent a great deal of the pregnancy in enforced bed rest. She now has a son, Daniel.

Kathryn runs the association as a data base for information on miscarriage – the kind of knowledge women need but which is not readily available. It aims to dispel the myths about miscarriage. Says Kathryn, 'Ignorance is not bliss when it causes so much fear and anxiety.'

It aims to make changes within the

medical profession in its attitude to miscarriage.

'We are only too aware of how over-worked doctors and medical staff are, but we still seek their support and advice.'

One big success has been the setting up of local groups, often with a leader who will encourage women to express their feelings freely, allow themselves to cry and grieve without being told they are being selfish or to 'shake themselves out of it'. Kathryn agrees with the sentiment expressed by a founder member when the organization was first set up: 'We want to give others the benefit of our own experiences and knowledge and to be to other women what we ourselves would have wanted had such a service been available at the time. Above all, we want to try to fill the gaps in the present system.'

'He lay on my hand. He was fully formed, perfect and beautiful. I was so thankful. I had seen him. Now I had something to focus my grief on.'

Heather Robertson is a living contradiction of the accepted woman of the Eighties. Not for her a slim figure, career and a freedom centred on the contraceptive pill, the easy abortion.

The first to admit that she is 'a large lady', Heather glides peacefully around her small, totally child-centred house in the unglamorous setting of Birmingham's inner city. The only view from her home is of the Midlands major motorway intersection known locally as 'Spaghetti Junction'. The only garden is a crammed back yard. But Heather is totally happy to have borne three children and made her family her priority. Her husband works in the stern grey world of the Midlands car industry. Heather's world centres around him and their three children. Her only grief – the three babies she lost through miscarriage.

An old-fashioned woman, her life didn't begin that way. She set out on a career, was actually trained as a ship's radio officer – 'But I never went to sea!' Calm and capable, her generous proportions give her a warm, motherly image. 'Let's face it, I'm fat. I was ashamed in hospital when it took four men to get me onto a trolley!'

The image may be modest and her ambitions now may be confined to the family, but Heather has brought tremendous comfort to women who have contacted her through the Miscarriage Association.

In the beginning, though, she was seeking help herself. It happened after her third miscarriage.

'I thought I was going mad! I had heard of the Miscarriage Association but they had just moved premises so it took me more than a day's pay in phone calls to find them. Birmingham to Yorkshire peak time – can you imagine the extravagance? But it was worth it. I talked with Kathryn Ladley and she told me I wasn't going mad. She gave me permission to grieve.

'At last, I had found someone who had felt as I did.

'Like so many women, I had come home to nothing. You go into hospital pregnant. You come out so quickly. It's been born, finished and taken away. Just a blank emptiness.

'They deal with you in hospital. You

have a D and C, they pat you on the head and there's an end to it. You come home to this awful emptiness, bewildered, confused, constantly asking yourself, "What have I done?" '

She speaks softly but her words are strong. 'Women are unjustifiably put down, kept in the dark about what has happened to them. My fight is against this terrible blanket of silence surrounding miscarriage. Doctors have probably learned very little about it except that a miscarriage is a routine, straight D and C. This demeans the child and the mother's experience.' Her anger stems from the time of her third miscarriage.

'I was sent home to take care of my other two children. No one spotted the dangers, that I tended to blame my two children for the loss of this child.

'I'd been told to rest in pregnancy when the miscarriage threatened.

'But with two tiny children at home, this had been impossible. I'd also been told not to pick them up – but I'd had to.

'Didn't it occur to anyone that I might take out my feelings on the children? Luckily, I didn't, but there was no follow-up visit from a midwife or health visitor. I felt totally alone.'

She feels a more realistic approach would help. 'At the best of times it's only a sixty–forty chance when you get pregnant that you'll come through with a live baby. Women are just not aware that when everyone is saying, "Congratulations – you are pregnant," that in fact their chances of a live baby are so slim.

'Everything in society is geared to success. We choose to have children. We choose the time. We want to be the perfect couple. We work, get our house together, have a couple of holidays abroad, then settle down and think, "Now we'll have our perfect little baby."

'Then suddenly it doesn't happen that way.

'For many women, this is the first time in their lives that they've failed at something. This is reinforced by a doctor saying, "Never mind. You can try again." In other words, you've failed this exam, but there's no reason why you can't take it again.

'The next time you fail for the second time. They still say, "Try again," but you feel totally let down. Your body has let you down and played an evil trick on you.

'There's no information. Let's face it, there's not a lot you can do. After all, you can't hold it in, stitch it back in again!

'In any case, most doctors will let an early miscarriage happen because of so many awful abnormalities in the foetuses.

'I don't blame the doctors. What incenses me is their lack of sympathy – in some cases there's none at all – and their unwillingness to discuss the miscarriage with the patient. For many of us, a D and C is our first operation. It's also our first dealing with death.

'You sit there so lost – I felt like a pickled cabbage – the first thought that crosses your mind is, "Will I be able to have any more children?" No one explains, no one reassures.

'One girl told me that her doctor did make an effort. He said to her, "You've come in with a nasty pain in your tummy, haven't you. We'll see what we can do about it, dear." He was talking to a grown woman!

'My consultant was a swine. A real swine, I had been nine weeks' pregnant when I started passing clots of blood. His junior saw me first – a terribly nice young doctor. The consultant said, "My dear, your uterus is sixteen weeks." I said "That's impossible. I cannot possibly be sixteen weeks pregnant." He ordered them to do a foetal trace. This is where they push an instrument over your stomach to pick up the heart-beat. The junior and nurse tried to do it, but didn't expect to find it. They didn't.

'The consultant came charging on to the ward at ten o'clock, when everyone was trying to settle down for the night.

'He pulled my sheets away, pulled back the curtains, threw off my covers, pulled up my nightie and slapped this instrument on to my stomach again. When he couldn't trace a heart-beat himself, he seemed extremely cross to be proved wrong. A scan and pregnancy test proved the baby was viable and I was told, "The baby is still alive. You can go home."

'I asked, "What about my bleeding? It's still going on. Does this mean I'm going to lose the baby or will I go on and have it?"

'The consultant glared at me. "I haven't got a crystal ball," he said and strode off.' Heather lost that baby at nearly fourteen weeks. She was in hospital as the miscarriage threatened and in a great deal of pain. 'The pain was mounting in intensity. It was worse than anything I had felt in childbirth. Of course, the pains would start in the middle of visiting time in a fourteen bed ward! My husband was sent away. I felt pains and the urge to push. A nurse drew the curtains and fetched Sister.

'I was left alone and I suddenly found myself touching my baby. It was such a shock when I realized it was a little body.

'I turned it over to discover it was a little boy. He was fully formed, perfect and beautiful with transparent skin.

'People have said to me afterwards, "You couldn't have known what sex he was," but I could see his sex organs, his little penis. I had another wave of pain then the tiny body was washed underneath with all the blood and clots. I was so afraid of crushing him that I daren't move. I had to stay like this till a doctor was called to inspect the mess.

'When Sister was allowed to clean it up, she held the body in her hand. "This might upset you," she said, but I said, "Let me look at him again." I looked at him and held him. That was enough for me. I'd seen him kicking on the scan. Now I had held him and seen him in Sister's hand. He looked so perfect, even beautiful. Now I had something to base my grief on. I knew the pregnancy had finished and I could come to terms with it. Normally in a miscarriage you don't see anything at all.

'With my previous two miscarriages I'd come home with all sorts of vague ideas in my mind, even after a D and C, that it might be all right after all and the baby would suddenly recover.

'You read such crazy things in newspapers that you go on kidding yourself for ages.

'The good thing to come out of Timothy's death was the support group in Birmingham. If I hadn't felt so lost when I came out of hospital, I would never have contacted the Miscarriage Association and been able to help so many people. To have seen him was just wonderful for me. I gave him a name – Timothy – and I blessed him. Now I can come to terms with his memory. It isn't going away. But in time it becomes less painful.'

CHAPTER 4

When a miscarriage happens

How much blood loss is normal? At what stage should you panic?

Alone in the house with my small daughter, my miscarriage got under way. The sharp abdominal pains were similar to giving birth. The blood loss grew heavier until it was impossible to stem with the usual sanitary towels and tampons. The inevitable was happening. I was losing the baby. How stupid I felt, not knowing what to expect. My midwife had trained me for childbirth, not for miscarriage. It wasn't something you talked about at relaxation classes. I should have been prepared. It had been a 'threatened miscarriage' for several days. I had read somewhere that you were supposed to keep the material which came away. The 'products of conception' were supposed to be preserved for a doctor to look at. But I couldn't imagine that any expert would gain much from looking at the clots of blood which were flowing from me. My mother had said, 'If you lose it, don't worry. It will be just like a lump of liver.'

There was one lump like that . . . was that the remains of the 'cluster of cells'

which had been my baby? Or was it the placenta? Whatever guessing games I played between cramping pains and surges of blood flow, one thing was certain. It didn't look much like Julia Frances!

I stood like a fool, fishing the 'lump of liver' out of the loo, inspected it without knowing what I was really looking for and decided in the end to flush it away . . . feeling, as the contractions died away, an overwhelming sense of physical relief. Contradicting all I felt mentally – for I had not wanted to lose the baby – my body just seemed to relax. The long weeks of waiting, praying, hoping against hope that I would not have a miscarriage, were all over. Physically I was just relieved.

This chapter is not for the squeamish. As one who was brought up to believe that menstruation, like defecation, is something that nice people don't talk about, I feel guilty for including it. Miscarriage, like the unlovelier parts of childbirth, should perhaps be whisked away, MGM-style, for the sake of our finer feelings. Close the bedroom door and leave the scene on a close-up of the husband looking worried . . . better if we don't know the details . . . better to 'try not to think about it.'

But women want to know. I wished that I had known what to expect.

I telephoned my doctor. For once, the receptionist didn't block my way to the busy man, but put me straight through. I felt very stupid. 'It's all right,' I said, having gone through the 'sorry to bother you' bit. 'I know it's a miscarriage and I can cope with it. It's just that I need to know how much blood loss to expect and when it gets dangerous. How much am I supposed to lose before I panic?' I laughed nervously, my GP and I having an unspoken agreement that, as long as my woes were neither crippling nor life threatening, we would attempt to make a joke of it.

He was good, my doctor. He said: 'You're a good girl and I know you can cope.

'But I think we'll have you in hospital, just to be on the safe side.'

That, bar all the shouting, was that. I was admitted to hospital, accompanied by a small girl who insisted on climbing into bed with me. Embarrassed I was, with all the blood and mess soiling the clean white hospital sheets. The medical team decided they would operate that night, a D and C would ensure that the uterus was completely empty. I was used to being in hospital in the night for Kathryn had been delivered by the night shift.

Two and a half years ago, I had watched the sun rise over Birmingham, knowing that she was safely born and asleep beside me. They don't sell postcards of the dawn over 'Brum', as it is lovingly known to all who live there! It is hardly a beauty spot. It had just seem-

ed beautiful to me, that morning, as light dawned on the high-rise flats and the factory yards. I was contented, having Kathryn, planning, even then, that I would have another. Having her had been easy. I suppose I took it for granted that her sister or brother would come just when I wanted them.

Other women had their families after years of good careers. It was the new social pattern to have babies late. You didn't have to start your family at 20 any more. So confident I was, having just produced my daughter. Now, having failed to produce anything at all, I didn't even bother to look out of the hospital window.

I just ate some hospital toast, my gynaecologist sent a thoughtful message to say how sorry he was, and I went home. People were kind, managed to say they were sorry, but it was probably 'all for the best'. Some kind of 'quality control' laid on by Mother Nature, I presumed, wondering just what kind of deformed monster they thought I had narrowly avoided giving birth to! One friend understood. 'Seems rotten luck to me,' she said. 'Wanting a baby for three years and then losing it!'

But nobody really said anything. It had been the great non-event of the year, I thought and, after a while, I started to cook. We had had a bumper crop of apples in the garden.

I devoted myself to apple pies, apple and blackberry puddings, apple crumbles, apple meringues . . . so that every time I went to the freezer, for months afterwards, I would pull out a dessert with a date on it to remind me of that week. Guests never knew that they were eating Miscarriage Pie . . .

One mistake I had made was to tell Kathryn very early that she could expect a brother or a sister. That meant telling her the bad news, too. She took it with three-year-old stoicism and mentioned it calmly to her nursery-school teacher. 'Mummy had a baby in her tummy but he died.'

That was my miscarriage, which was followed by three more miscarriages in the following year. They were so early I hardly had time to know I was pregnant. I had only the Positive Pregnancy Test certificates from the pharmacists as evidence that they had been – and they had all gone by twelve weeks. What shall I do with all the certificates, I asked myself. Paper the bedroom wall with them? Evidence of what might have been . . .

It comes as a shock

Everyone's experience of miscarriage is different. I was lucky in that I had had a threatened miscarriage for some weeks and was prepared for it. For Denise, a full-time polytechnic student doing a course in Humanities, the loss of a baby came as a complete shock. She is angry about the way she was treated.

'Why was I treated so brutally? They left me shattered, devastated and a sobbing wreck. Wasn't there a more considerate way to tell me that my baby was dead?'

DENISE, aged 31, was happily expecting her fourth baby. Twenty weeks' pregnant, she went to the hospital for a routine scan, accompanied by her family, including her two younger sons aged seven and ten. Afterwards they were going to a wedding.

'We were joking with the two boys about the baby we were expecting. I felt sure it would be a boy and they had christened him Jethro. I had felt him kicking. The girl in the scan room came out to greet us and cheerfully told them that they would soon see "their little brother on television!"

'I was asked to go in first. They told me they were using a new machine and asked whether I would mind the presence of an engineer, which of course I didn't.

'It soon became obvious that the girl was having trouble with the ultrasound picture of the baby on the screen. She fiddled about with it and said she thought there was a fault with the machine. She went off to fetch a doctor but couldn't find one.

'They put us all out in the waiting area. It served the entire X-ray department, so all kinds of patients were there.

'I was still wearing that awful loose gown you have to put on for a scan. Then a registrar arrived and announced, "I'm afraid your baby is dead." This was almost casually said, in full hearing of the entire family, including the children.

'I will never forget their faces. They just couldn't get over the shock.

'The registrar gave me a scrap of paper with instructions to take it to a ward in two days' time for a D and C. He went off. Luckily my partner Stuart was with me and I was left clinging to him, sobbing. I just didn't know what the doctor had been talking about. One minute I was happily pregnant and we were looking forward to the arrival of Jethro – then this! It was a nightmare.

'We abandoned plans to attend the wedding and went straight home, trying to answer the boys' questions. Of course, at twenty weeks, to talk of a D and C was nonsense, anyway. At that stage the baby would have had to be induced.

'I started to lose the baby naturally the night before I was due to go into hospital. An hour and a half of labour and I delivered him. We rang for an ambulance but it didn't make it before the baby was born.

'He was perfect. Stuart and I held him for a while and then took him to the hospital for a post-mortem. I had to battle to persuade them to release him for burial, as it was only twenty weeks' gestation.

'The hospital had me back for a D and C but there was no doctor around to tell me anything. In the end, the hospital chaplain was helpful in organizing the burial.

'I was so glad we had a funeral. It was a lovely sunny day. My sons came with us. My eldest, 14, had been knitting the baby a blanket so he put it with the body and my smallest son put his teddy in, saying that it was about the same size as Jethro.

'It was a lovely garden where the baby was buried. A squirrel was playing. The flowers were beautiful. It was something for us all to remember.

'It makes me angry to think of the way the hospital told me. I'm not resentful of the baby's death. That couldn't have been avoided. But there was no need for the cold brutality I received. They could at least have taken the children away for five minutes while they told me.'

Miscarriage: a man's reaction

'A miscarriage either makes or breaks a relationship. That's what the midwife told me at the time. In our case it brought us closer and we now have a much deeper relationship.'

When DENISE lost her baby at twenty weeks, STUART was '... devastated. Being told so abruptly that the baby was dead was shattering. I've tried to understand why the guy did it like that. He was probably tired after a long shift. I do know how hard doctors work. But to come out with it like that in front of the children was all wrong.'

Denise had to drive the family home as Stuart does not drive. 'It was a hideous experience coming home to a different reality. We had set off so happily for the wedding. Now it was all over.

'We have some understanding friends who took the boys away for the day, as I don't think we could have coped with the normal routine of meals, etc.

'When she started to miscarry in the early hours of the morning, I went into the bathroom with her. It was two hours before she was due to go into hospital. The baby came away. Jethro was a perfect little boy, with long limbs, fingernails and an incredibly peaceful face. He was so serene.

'I had worked with ambulances and in a burns unit for a time, so death itself was nothing new to me. But it was my first experience of death in someone of my blood, so close.

'It was amazing how we did everything by instinct. Den cut the cord herself while I held Jethro and put him into a jug to take to the hospital.

'I was so glad to have seen him. Afterwards I just wanted to stay near Den, even when she was asleep.

'When she came out of hospital and was recovering at home, I was doing the shopping and found that friends would ask, "How's Den?" as if they didn't think I had suffered a loss at all but I felt it deeply. I felt completely powerless. Always before in my life I had been able to do something in a given situation. In this one I could do nothing. I couldn't bring him back to life.

'I wanted to turn the clock back to when we were that happy little family party off to a wedding and calling at the hospital to make sure our baby was all right – just a routine scan.

'I don't want to demean Jethro's life and death in any way, but the fact is that the way we lost him, at home and both of us able to see him, has made a close relationship much, much deeper.

'We have no particular religious faith, but we both feel that sometimes Jethro, that gentle-looking little Jethro, is close to us.

'It is very important to me that he was buried, as that garden is a place I can go to remember him and feel him close.

'Our friends have been wonderful but we both feel that we have been in our own world since he died and in a way cut off from them.

'It has made me appreciate the fleeting nature of life. That one minute life is fun and we are off to a wedding. The next minute death has come suddenly and our lives have fallen to pieces . . .'

Denise went back to the hospital for a follow-up visit. 'Things were no better. A young houseman asked whether this had been my first pregnancy and started advocating a cervical stitch.

'He obviously hadn't even read my notes. This was my fourth pregnancy, not my first! As for putting in a cervical stitch, that was nonsense as there had been no question of cervical incompetence. I had to tell him that it had been an intra-uterine death.

'He told me to understand that he saw hundreds of miscarriages every week. I couldn't believe the nightmare of it all. There I was, having had the worst, most devastating experience of my life and a bored young doctor was telling me that it was nothing.'

Denise felt that the only person in the hospital who was really helpful was the porter. 'He tried to find out about funeral arrangements for us. He even rang us at home!'

Many women are aware, as I was, of their own ignorance about miscarriage. This is something which worried KATE a great deal: '*Why didn't any doctor tell me what to do when I had a miscarriage? How was I to know when a blood loss was normal – or dangerous?*'

Kate is not stupid. A teacher by profession, she was keen to do everything to make sure her pregnancy went well. Other things in her life had been successful. Her husband Nick had a good job as a video engineer. They had bought the house they wanted. Now they both wanted a baby. They were all ready, until suddenly Kate found herself bleeding heavily – a miscarriage was starting.

Slim, clear-eyed and scrubbed clean as her shining new house, Kate had found out she was pregnant on her thirty-first birthday.

'I had conceived as soon as we wanted a baby. It was great.'

Kate and Nick had taken the trouble to consult her doctor before going in for a child. As a fifteen-year-old, an accident on a school trampoline had damaged her back and she knew she would one day need an operation. 'My consultant said that surgery could wait and advised me to have a pregnancy first. I wanted to have a baby straightaway. Thirty-one is a bit old to have a first baby.'

She was examined by her gynaecologist at nine weeks. 'He is nice. Friendly, chatty. He said, "The baby is fine. Now relax and enjoy the pregnancy." His only little comment was that my breasts didn't seem to be enlarged. But there was nothing to worry about.'

However, Kate did worry. 'I was so scared, frightened of anything which might harm the baby. I was always poring over books on babies, magazine features, newspapers . . . every day there was something new to worry about.

'I read somewhere that the microwave in the kitchen could be a hazard and I wouldn't go near it.

'I called round at a neighbour's house and discovered their child had chickenpox. I was worried sick that I might catch it and damage the baby in the same way that rubella (German measles) can cause blindness and deafness. All in all, the pregnancy was one long nightmare instead of being the happy time it should have been.'

Kate and Nick made it a rule to be careful what they ate and not to drink alcohol. 'Then we were invited to a bonfire party. To be on the safe side, we both watched the fireworks from inside so that I didn't get cold. We didn't drink much – only non-alcoholic lager – and we didn't smoke. Some people were drinking too much and making themselves ill, but not us.'

Unfortunately, they ate some barbecue food. 'Because it was party food, it was all mixed up, dips and things, so you don't really know what you are eating.

'I had been careful to avoid goat's milk and cheese, which I normally have to help my back pain, because my mother had warned me it might be bad for the baby. But this was before the government panic on soft cheeses and there had been no official warnings at the time. It was getting to be a bit of a wild party so we went home early. During the night I woke up feeling unwell, with an awful heavy feeling. By 8 a.m. I wanted to be sick and knew something was wrong.

'I was sick and vomiting all day. My sister suggested an aspirin to bring down my temperature but I daren't take any drugs for fear of harming the baby. Everyone said, "Don't worry. Your illness won't harm the pregnancy," but I knew a high temperature wasn't good for it and that worried me most.'

By Monday, Kate's fever had broken

but as soon as she stood up, bleeding began. On the telephone, her GP commented: 'It sounds like a threatened miscarriage to me.'

'When he said that I felt really wretched.

'I rang my mother who cheered me up by saying it was only happening because I was depressed and it would be all right.'

She saw her gynaecologist. 'He was all reassurance until I said, "I don't feel pregnant anymore," at which he changed swiftly and booked a scan for me, five days ahead.'

But Kate didn't make it to the appointment. On Saturday, still feeling ill, she attempted to help Nick decorate the house. She was lethargic and miserable. 'We ended up having a row. I was losing a lot more blood so I asked him to fetch us a video tape to take my mind off things. He came with, would you believe, a film called *Death Wish Four*!

'I said, "Well done. Just what I needed to cheer me up!" We had words and the bleeding got really heavy. I knew than that a miscarriage was going to happen. We had a copy of Miriam Stoppard's book on having a baby and went to bed, reading it, hoping it would give us a clue on what to do. My GP hadn't given me any idea what I might expect. I still didn't know whether I would keep it or whether it would die.

'I don't know what's normal, how much blood you are supposed to lose. Suddenly, there was a great big contraction. Nick came with me into the bathroom. In the book it had emphasized that you were supposed to keep what comes away for the doctor to see, so Nick dived downstairs and grabbed a paint pot. It was all right, he'd cleaned it up. It sounds funny really, the panic we were in!

'The baby came away into that. It was about the size of a hen's egg. I was shaking and I daren't look.' A telephone call to the doctor was an afterthought. 'We were starting to go back to bed when I suddenly thought perhaps I had better ring the doctor. He got me straight into hospital and they kept me in for a D and C. The staff at the hospital said it was a good thing we had rung. It was essential to let them know as I might have had a haemorrhage. I was angry then. Why had no one told me I could have been in danger?'

Nick feels the experience has given him new confidence.

'I never thought I would be able to cope with a situation like that – the most awful thing I could imagine. My wife in pain in the middle of all that blood and mess. But I found I could cope with it. I could even discern the shape of a foetus in that undignified paint pot. I wasn't as squeamish as I had imagined. On the whole, I think it has brought us close together.'

Kate is still upset because her pregnancy was ruined by the worry about possible hazards. 'I should have been happy, but I wasn't. I spent the whole pregnancy worrying about one thing after another . . . there were so many danger warnings in the press. Now they are telling us that we can get listeria food poisoning from cheeses and that eggs are dangerous.'

CAROL, who lost her baby because she suffered listeria food poisoning was shocked by the tragedy. 'It was awful to have to deliver a dead baby. When they knew the baby was dead I was induced and in labour for four and a half hours. Luckily, my husband and mother were very supportive. I knew that the baby was a boy but I didn't want to see him. It would have been imprinted on my brain forever if I had once looked at him.

'This happened to me before it was in all the papers and I had had no idea of the dangers of eating certain foods. But in any case I never ate soft cheeses. Doctors explained to us that it could be in the soil around us, even in animals, but in the end we put it down to pre-chilled meat.

'Ever since I have tried to eat carefully. Instead of a boiled egg and toast, I would just have toast! I got so worried I just didn't know what to eat and ended up living on toast and water!'

Carol's worst moment came six months later when the UK Government began to put out warnings about listeria in cheese and salmonella in eggs.

'By that time I was pregnant again. I was horrified. How I got through the last few weeks of pregnancy I will never know. I ended up just drinking water.'

Carol's luck was in, however, and she gave birth to a healthy daughter, Nicola.

'She has had full tests and is fine. But because it upset me so much I write a lot of features in local newspapers and go on local radio to tell other women to be careful about their food.

'If I were pregnant again, I would avoid eggs completely and soft cheeses; also take care with pre-chilled meats. I am breast-feeding now so I follow those rules myself. It is far too great a risk.'

Well, what is the truth about food dangers to expectant mums? How much should we worry? Can we *prevent* a miscarriage? In the next chapter, a few guidelines to help you . . .

CHAPTER 5

How to avoid it in the first place

So you are pregnant. Great. But you've read about all the things that can go wrong and you're frankly terrified. Instead of enjoying your pregnancy, you are worried sick!

Who can blame you? We are cautioned on so many dangers these days that it is a wonder any expected baby survives the first three months!

KATE is typical of the new wave of intelligent, well-read women who want to do their very best for the health of an expected baby. She read every medical article in sight and ransacked the library for more. Her husband backed her up and they set out on the great adventure of their lives – having a baby.

The problem was, they found there were so many things which could go wrong that it became a miserable few weeks. 'Every week something would crop up to worry us and become *this week's worry*!' says Nick. 'We were anxious about being in contact with infection, about the microwave in the kitchen, and, above all, what we were eating and drinking. Life became a real trial.'

Their pregnancy ended sadly but they are embarking on a further one with much enthusiasm. Kate has already decided to give up eating eggs in view of the salmonella scare.

There are many other young couples as well meaning and worried as Kate and Nick. But should expectant mums inflict such misery on themselves?

Dr Barbara Pickard is a leading authority on pregnancy and nutrition.[4] She is horrified to see the current hysteria in the media. 'It alarms me that so many warnings are being given out these days. The last thing we should be doing is worrying pregnant women, because the worry in itself is likely to cause stress.'

Dr Pickard combines a busy life as an honorary university Research Fellow, with bringing up four children and running a small Yorkshire hill farm. She has written many academic papers on care in pregnancy. Nowadays, however, her commitment is primarily to her family and her professional life is 'strictly part-time'.

She says: 'Eggs are a very important part of our diet and it grieves me that people are cutting them out simply because of the Government warnings on salmonella. In fact, if you get them from the same supplier you always have there is no reason whatsoever why you should make changes. I don't think a government can start telling us that every egg should be hard-boiled. It is up to the individual to make her own decision.'

In the UK, the Government's Medical Officer has also suggested that pregnant women should avoid certain types of soft cheeses, including soft ripened cheese such as Brie, Camembert and blue-vein cheese. These are thought to contain high counts of the bacterium *Listeria monocytogenes*. The bacteria have the unusual property of being able to multiply at the temperature found in domestic refrigerators. They have also been found in pre-cooked, ready-to-eat poultry and cooked and chilled meals which need reheating before consumption.

Dr Pickard feels that 'listeria hysteria' should not prevent a pregnant woman enjoying her food! She recommends: 'Go back to being an old-fashioned housekeeper – the kind who knows which foods keep and which don't, how to keep food properly stored in a big, airy larder, even when you don't have refrigeration. Shop as often as possible, so that food is *fresh*.

'Make up your own mind what you're going to eat, having read the facts.'

Listeria surrounds us daily. It is found in soil, vegetation and the faeces of man and animal, so some exposure is inevitable. At any time, around one person in twenty carries the bacteria without any apparent ill-effects.

If you are pregnant, follow these rules of preparation:

1   Heat ready-to-eat poultry and cook chilled meals until they are piping hot.
2   Respect the 'Best by' and 'Eat by' dates on the label.
3   Don't eat undercooked poultry. Don't eat undercooked meat products.
4   Make sure the fridge works. It will only keep the food really cold if you defrost it often. Don't wait for it to look like the Antarctic with frozen ice!

ELAINE, 32, nearly lost her baby through listeria. She says: 'It was touch and go. If it hadn't been for the skill of the doctors and the fact that I was in a big city hospital with wonderful laboratory facilities, I don't think my baby would be here today.'

She feels strongly that pregnant women should be wary of what they eat. 'I was very lucky. But I am most careful now about the food I eat, particularly pre-cooked chilled chicken. I go cold with horror when I think what might have happened.'

It was Christmas 1986 and Elaine's first baby was nearly due. She was 32 weeks' pregnant, so had a quiet holiday, taking things easily through Christmas and New Year. Her only evening out was a restaurant curry on New Year's Eve.

Shortly afterwards she was taken violently ill with a raging temperature and 'flu symptoms. 'I felt really ill and within three hours of the illness starting I went into labour, feeling very ill throughout a quick labour.'

When her daughter Amy was born she weighed only 4 lbs 6 oz (1.98 kg).

At 4 a.m. nurses woke Elaine to tell her that the baby was in trouble.

'They had noticed that she was very cold. The doctor was called and they gave her blood tests every half hour and a lumbar puncture. They were able to identify it as a listeria bug and do all the right things. But as this was only New Year 1987, there had been no warning of a listeria scare and they were really groping for information. They kept on asking me whether I had been in contact with animals – in the middle of a big city, I had to tell them I hadn't been near sheep or cattle!

'They had such a battle to save her life. I'm sure that if I'd been at a smaller hospital I wouldn't have her now. I'll be eternally grateful. Amy is now two. When her brother was born, he had to undergo listeria tests. Luckily, he was fine. But I am more than careful now about the food I eat. It was such a shock. You really can't be too careful!'

So: **Play safe!**

1 Adopt a healthy diet (see Chapter 17).
2 Avoid contact with German measles (rubella) unless you were immunized against it before you became pregnant.
3 Make sure you are not working with toxic chemicals (see list in Chapter 16).
4 Cut out the following:
 (a) Excessive alcohol. A recent report from Dr Maurice Kaufman of Cambridge University drew attention to 'the potential danger to the unborn baby of a single episode of heavy drinking at about the time of conception'. The damage caused was likely to result in miscarriage, according to Dr Kaufman. But it was *heavy* drinking, so don't start worrying about that one glass of wine!
 (b) Smoking. The risk of miscarriage increases directly with increasing levels of maternal smoking, according to Dr D.U. Himmelberger writing in the *American Journal of Epidemiology*, who also found that smokers miscarry more normal foetuses than non-smokers.

Smokers are also more likely to have live births of babies with congenital abnormalities such as cleft palates and hare lips. Approximately one third of women smoke (30 per cent of women in the USA and 37 per cent in the UK). Smoking among younger women has increased.

Smoking is often associated with miscarriages (Huisjes)[5]

 (c) Drugs. Everyone knows, by now, the disastrous effects which drugs can have on the delicate foetus, which can be tragically deformed. Thalidomide is the classic example, resulting in thousands of babies born in the early 1960s without arms and legs. It has now been shown that some benzodiazepines – tranquillizers – if taken during the first three months of pregnancy, may also cause babies to be deformed. Many mums-to-be do take tranquillizers. A recent survey of 156 American expectant mothers showed that one in four of them had taken tranquillizers at some time during pregnancy.

So simply cut out all drugs – illegal, prescribed, even the aspirin

bought over the counter in the pharmacy. **Don't take it unless your doctor, knowing you are pregnant, prescribes it for you.**

(d) Medical X-rays. It is unlikely that you will be X-rayed at a hospital (except in emergencies) when you are newly pregnant. It is also standard practice to X-ray a woman of child-bearing age only during the first ten days of her cycle although some experts feel that even with this precaution a developing egg could be damaged. Just to be on the safe side, don't have an X-ray at all when you are either pregnant or 'trying' for a baby.

Just to be on the safe side, don't have an X-ray at the dentists.

5 Avoid the following:

(a) Elderly microwave ovens. There is evidence to show that certain microwave ovens 'leak' when they get old, and allow electromagnetic radiation to escape. Microwaves are known to affect the reproductive organs in close proximity. Please note that this only means you avoid an old microwave – I am sure yours is *new*, in perfect order, and there is no chance that it will leak!

(b) Visual Display Units (VDUs). Difficult if you work in an office, but once you are pregnant, you can ask your employer to allow you not to work with one during the first twelve weeks. Otherwise, not more than four hours' VDU work a day is recommended.

VDUs emit an electric and magnetic field due to their high voltage electrical components. Sitting three feet (approximately one metre) from a VDU screen, eight hours a day, five days a week, may cause a wide variety of problems, including an increased rate of miscarriages, back-ache, eye strain and stress.

6 Don't – whatever you do – go on a slimming diet! This is the one time in your life when it is not a good idea to lose weight, even if you are somewhat overweight when you start the pregnancy. A sensible eating plan (such as one devised by Weight Watchers) is OK, but now is *not* the time to take up the lettuce-leaf diet or the diet which consists of three grapefruits and a banana a day.

Be sensible! Researchers working on the effects of war-time starvation in the 1940s found that there were many deaths and malformations among the babies conceived at that time. A drastic diet may put your developing baby into the same situation!

7 Above all, avoid getting stressed. Having taken as many precautions as you can to prevent miscarriage and maintain your pregnancy, please don't let yourself get into a state of permanent worrying about it. The risks are there, but they are minimal and the chances of your being affected by the things I've listed are very small indeed.

So *relax*! The doctors are not just wishing you to have a good time when they tell you to enjoy the pregnancy. A happy pregnancy really will make for a successful outcome. So keep cheerful, tranquil – what's wrong with a bit of knitting? If you feel yourself getting agitated, you can always turn to yoga for relaxation or even homoeopathy.

KAY, who has had one miscarriage, didn't want her second pregnancy to go the same way, so she consulted a homoeopath. 'The problem was I was vomiting a lot in early pregnancy and was also getting very anxious,' says Kay. 'The homoeopath gave me one tiny tablet and the effects lasted two or three weeks. No sickness and I stopped worrying. I was also advised to take plenty of calcium.'

If the worst happens and you have a miscarriage

What do you do? How do you cope? How will you know that it is a miscarriage?

When it began for me, the only symptom was a very slight loss of brownish blood. Unexpected, because in my previous pregnancy, there hadn't been a spot of blood for nine months.

If this happens with you, you may find it worrying, ominous, and suddenly find yourself paying endless visits to the loo to check up.

Am I bleeding? Is it getting worse? What do I do? Is it silly to make a fuss? Do other women get the same thing?

Well, yes they do. Many women get bleeding in pregnancy and it means nothing. They go on to have fine, healthy babies. On the other hand, early bleeding can be a sign that something is wrong.

JENNY, a secretary, said: 'I had had one miscarriage and I was terrified it would happen with the next pregnancy. When I bled heavily, just like a period, I thought, "That's it!" But it wasn't.

'The baby was fine and the pregnancy continued normally.'

A miscarriage is a foetus lost in pregnancy at any time before the 28th week. Most happen before the fourteenth week.

If all goes according to plan

If all is going well, about midway between periods a woman releases an egg from her ovary which is fertilized by a male sperm, through sexual intercourse.

The two cells fuse – a process which is known, of course, as conception. Cell division takes place and a cluster of cells, rather like a bunch of grapes, is formed.

Two thirds of this cluster become the embryo – the start of the developing baby (see Figure 1). A third of it becomes the placenta, which is the organ which acts as filter for food and oxygen. It remains attached to the embryo by a rope of blood vessels. A bag, rather like a polythene bag, grows over the placenta and the baby lives inside it. The placenta secretes water and the baby floats inside the bag (amniotic sac). This water protects it and acts as a buffer. If all is not well, the entire contents of the womb must be expelled in miscarriage.

These products of conception must leave the body.

In a miscarriage, will I actually lose a dead person?

Before the 28th week, the developing

foetus and the rest of the contents of the womb are known medically as the 'products of conception' and have no legal status. After the 28th week, it is classed medically as a still-birth and the death is normally registered.

However, developments in medicine now mean that a baby born much younger – at, say, 26 weeks – can sometimes survive with intensive care so these definitions may be revised.

Figure 1
When all goes according to plan

You are eight weeks pregnant. The early 'baby', the embryo, is about one inch long, but safe in its protective amniotic sac (bag of waters). The cervix is safely closed. The placenta is developing as a food store.

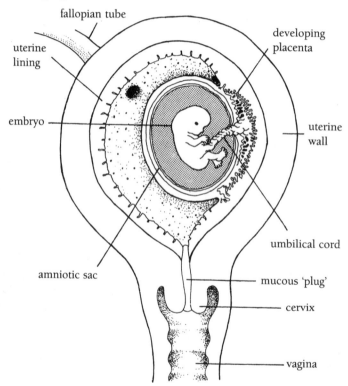

fallopian tube

uterine lining

developing placenta

embryo

uterine wall

umbilical cord

amniotic sac

mucous 'plug'

cervix

vagina

Why do doctors call a miscarriage an abortion?

The word miscarriage is very much a lay person's term. In medicine this is known as a spontaneous abortion, while a deliberate abortion is known as

an elective abortion, i.e. one you choose to have. This term can cause tremendous offence. Christine, who is highly religious and a member of the Pentecostal Church, was horrified when a new doctor, reading her notes, said, 'I see here that you have had an abortion.' Christine was furious.

She had in fact had a miscarriage. She refused to be mollified by the doctor's explanation that it was 'just a medical term' and insisted, 'If that is in my notes you can delete it straightaway – while I am here.'

Why do most miscarriages occur before the sixteenth week? It is not really known why, but there does seem to be a 'cut-off' point at sixteen weeks, after which women feel more confident, more 'safe' from having a miscarriage. It may be related to the vital change-over point when the placenta takes over the role of food store.

Until then, a gland called the corpus luteum is responsible. It could be that the corpus luteum fails to provide adequate hormones before the placenta is ready to start work.

Why do most women have to have a D and C operation after a miscarriage

A miscarriage may not harm your body at all. Many women conceive and lose babies without even knowing it, perhaps putting it down to a period which seems a little heavy or a couple of days late. Many women don't even contact their doctors. But the dangers of miscarriage are that there could be severe bleeding (haemorrhage) or infection afterwards. This happens if all the tissue (all the products of conception) have not been expelled from the womb. The D and C 'scrapes' the womb with an instrument known as a curette.

What happens if you have a late miscarriage, i.e. after sixteen weeks?

There are a few miscarriages between sixteen and 28 weeks. They involve hospitalization and the delivery of a dead baby. But only a tiny percentage of miscarriages happen this late.

Should you always contact your doctor if you think you are miscarrying?

Says Heather Robertson, who runs a Birmingham group for the Miscarriage Association: 'We always advise mums to ring their doctor, tell him what's happening, put plenty of protection – perhaps newspaper – on the sheets, and lie down. We also mention that it's a good idea to have an overnight case packed in case of going into hospital. It helps a woman to be given something to do. It saves her from wandering around the house in a panic.

Does it hurt to have a miscarriage?

'Yes. It hurts like hell.'

'No. It hardly hurt me physically at all. It was no worse than a heavy period.'

Both these answers are true but they come from different women. As in childbirth, each woman's experience is different.

JOANNE, who lost a baby at twelve weeks, said: 'It hurt much more than having a baby. I had to beg the nurse to give me pain-killers.'

LIZ, losing her third child, reported that no one understood when she commented in hospital on the 'pain' of the experience: 'I meant that it was hurtful emotionally to lose the baby I wanted so much. The nurses didn't understand

and gave me pethidine.'

The best way to describe the sensation of miscarriage is that the pains, as in childbirth, are uterine contractions. Just how much they hurt depends on the individual woman's tolerance of pain and how far the pregnancy has progressed. It is very much a mini-labour if it happens at say, 22 weeks, but only 3 per cent of miscarriages are late ones (between fourteen and 28 weeks of pregnancy).

The average miscarriage happens before sixteen weeks and women have described the pain as 'hardly hurting at all'.

'Fast contractions coming rapidly as though I was about to deliver a live baby.'

'Agony. I had to convince the staff how much it was hurting. They accused me of being ridiculous and making it up.'

When a miscarriage begins, there may be low abdominal and back pain, slight brownish spotting or bright red blood, the ominous heralds of an impending period. Your doctor may suggest bed rest. There is no real evidence that this does any good. But it does no harm. MARGARET, starting to miscarry a third pregnancy, decided on a definite policy: 'I felt the only way was to become a slut.

'Normally, as I live in the country, I would get out the estate car and dash into the nearest town for a big super-market shop. I would run the children to school, swimming classes, ballet, Brownies . . . I felt that if I pushed on at this pace, I might well make things worse and lose the baby. So I became a slut. I shopped locally – expensively – at the village shop. I shamelessly recruited my friends to pick up the children and persuaded my husband to take them to school. I just had to put my feet up as the one chance of keeping the baby.' Sadly, however, Margaret miscarried at thirteen weeks. 'The bed rest hadn't made much difference. At least, though, I feel I did my best to hang on to the pregnancy.'

Once a miscarriage has begun, can anything be done to save the baby?

No. Some doctors believe that a miscarriage can be avoided if the woman is injected with natural progesterone but this treatment is controversial (see Chapter 14).

If the cervix (the neck or entrance to the womb) is open you will lose the baby.

The cervix is normally closed throughout pregnancy, as the safe door which keeps the baby secure.

Once it opens you will miscarry. This is what the doctor calls an 'inevitable' miscarriage. You won't know whether your cervix is open. Your doctor will.

Figure 2   The blighted ovum pregnancy   ➤

You are eight weeks pregnant. The sac and placenta are developing normally, as in Figure 1. But the baby – the embryo – has died at an early basic stage. A miscarriage is inevitable.

Are there different types of miscarriage?

Yes. You may have a 'missed' miscarriage, where the foetus has failed to develop properly – or had developed and then died. The mother may not notice that anything is wrong, perhaps only slight spotting of blood. As this has not been spontaneously expelled as a miscarriage, it must be removed by a D and C.

This is one of the cruellest kinds of miscarriage as the mother may go for an antenatal appointment believing that all is well, only to be told that the pregnancy is over, the baby is dead.

How will I know whether my baby is alive?

The most useful piece of equipment for a doctor is the ultrasound scan in which sound-waves give him or her a picture of what is happening inside the uterus. This way the doctor can tell whether there are any signs of life.

The first scan may be inconclusive but a later one will show up the truth.

A blighted ovum

This occurs when the early cluster of cells never develops beyond a very basic stage and the amniotic sac is vir-

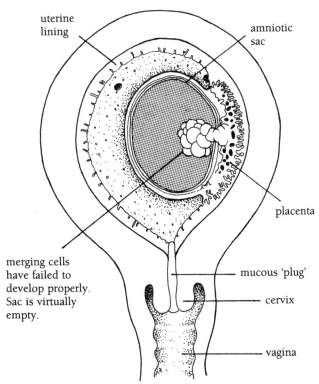

uterine lining

amniotic sac

placenta

merging cells have failed to develop properly. Sac is virtually empty.

mucous 'plug'

cervix

vagina

tually empty (see Figure 2). The mother may bleed at around nine weeks, then again two or three weeks later. This may be just a small amount and she may wonder whether it is anything to worry about at all.

This is a sad situation where all the physical needs for the baby have developed. He has a placenta, a sac – a complete 'nursery' in the woman's body. She is pregnant, with the usual morning sickness and enlarged breasts. But the most important person of all in this preparation – the baby – has 'died', failed completely to BE at all.

A miscarriage is inevitable. When such a pregnancy is diagnosed, doctors will usually perform a D and C operation to avoid the risk of spontaneous abortion and possible infection.

A complete miscarriage

In a *complete* miscarriage everything has come away – foetus, sac and placenta. Doctors have to make sure that this has happened. If it is incomplete, a woman may go on bleeding after the miscarriage and this could cause infection.

A hydatidiform mole miscarriage

Another type of miscarriage is the hydatidiform mole miscarriage. The placenta develops normally but usually no foetus is present.

The rise in hormone levels with the increased size of the placenta means that the woman feels very sick. Usually a 'mole' pregnancy will miscarry spontaneously, but if it does not a D and C must be done. In very rare cases (about 10 per cent) a form of cancer called choriocarcinoma may develop. So women are given frequent check-ups after a mole pregnancy and advised against a further baby for at least a year.

Miscarriage due to hormonal insufficiency

Hormonal insufficiency can result in miscarriage. For the first fourteen weeks, the baby is fed through the corpus luteum, a gland formed from the ruptured egg sac on the ovary (see Figure 3). The corpus luteum produces oestrogen and progesterone – hormones which build up the lining of the womb. It must carry on with this work until the placenta takes over at the vital take-over point of fourteen weeks. If it fails to produce sufficient hormone until then, or the placenta doesn't 'take over' adequately, miscarriage may occur. This is sometimes known as 'placental insufficiency'.

Cervical incompetence

An incompetent cervix could be the cause of miscarriage. Sometimes the cervix (neck or entrance of the womb) doesn't stay safely closed to contain the baby.

It opens too soon (dilates) and causes a later miscarriage – often after sixteen weeks (see Figure 4). This can be overcome medically by the insertion of a cervical stitch (the Shirodkar or Macdonald Suture, named after the doctors who introduced them).

The stitch (in fact, a surgical tape is used) is inserted in early pregnancy, or before, if the problem is known about with a previous pregnancy. The stitch is removed at about 38 weeks. It is always

Figure 3 Hormonal insufficiency

Twelve weeks pregnant. The baby is now two inches long and developing rapidly. If the lips are stroked, it will close the mouth tightly and swallow. At this stage the vital takeover happens when the food source is no longer the corpus luteum but the placenta. If the corpus luteum fails before the placenta is ready to take over a miscarriage due to hormonal deficiency can occur.

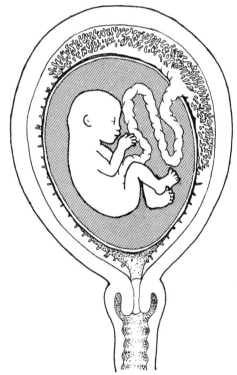

done under general anaesthetic.

Abnormal womb shape

A strangely shaped womb can sometimes cause a miscarriage. Many women have a uterus which is not the normal 'pear' shape (see Figure 5). It does not necessarily mean they will miscarry, but occasionally the particular shape does not leave enough room for the baby to grow properly; for instance, in the womb which has a sep-

tum – a membrane dividing it right down the middle.

Ectopic pregnancy

An ectopic pregnancy happens when the foetus grows in the wrong place! Usually it develops in the fallopian tube instead of implanting in the womb in the normal way (see Figure 6). If it is not diagnosed, the tube may burst – an extremely dangerous medical situation.

It is believed that an ectopic pregnan-

Figure 4 Cervical incompetence

Normally the cervix (neck of the womb) remains firmly closed for nine months, holding the contents of the womb quite safely. But sometimes the cervix releases the contents much too early, allowing the baby to be expelled before it can possibly survive.

(a) Competent (normal) cervix

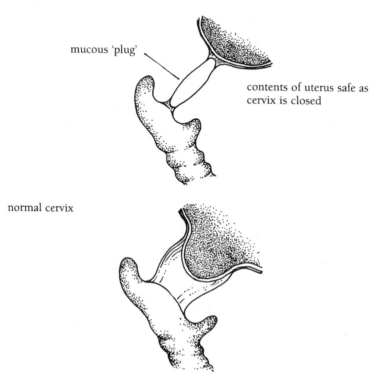

mucous 'plug'

contents of uterus safe as cervix is closed

normal cervix

(b) Incompetent cervix

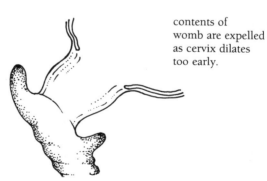

contents of womb are expelled as cervix dilates too early.

Figure 5 Abnormal womb shape

(a) The normal uterus

(b) Uterus with septum in the middle (this can make it difficult for the developing baby to have enough room to grow)

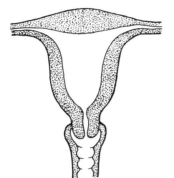

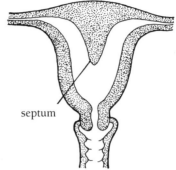

septum

(c) Bi-cornate (two-horned) uterus

(d) Uni-cornate (one-horned) uterus

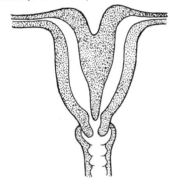

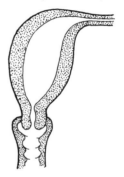

cy can be caused by the intra-uterine device or previous pelvic infection. The foetus is removed by surgery.

Incompatible blood groups

Things can go wrong when a rhesus-negative woman is carrying a rhesus-positive child.

During the pregnancy or birth rhesus-positive blood cells can escape from the baby into the mother's bloodstream.

The mother's body recognizes the cells as foreign and is sensitized to pro-duce antibodies against them the next time it encounters such cells – *next* time, but not immediately. So it isn't until she has her second rhesus-positive baby that she faces trouble. When this baby releases cells into the mother's bloodstream they meet cir-culating antibodies which were previously produced. The antibodies cross the placenta and enter the baby's body where they start destroying red cells, producing severe anaemia and heart failure likely to kill the baby.

Figure 6   Ectopic pregnancy

Sometimes the embryo implants in the wrong place, usually the Fallopian tube. This is called an ectopic pregnancy and can occur in the wider or narrower parts of the tube. If the Fallopian tube bursts the pain can be agonizing and is a real medical emergency.

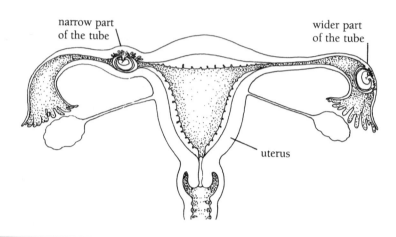

narrow part of the tube

wider part of the tube

uterus

Luckily, this is not such a big problem as it was twenty years ago, because doctors have worked out a way of dealing with it. Anti-D-gamma-globulin can be injected into these women so that they do not form antibodies.

An important question which worries women after miscarriage is: *Did I lose the baby because it was handicapped or deformed?*

This, of course, is the great message of consolation given freely to women who have miscarried. 'It's nature's way,' everyone tells you.

A kind of well-intentioned quality control set up by the Almighty to prevent us giving birth to babies we might not like the look of . . . or who might not expect much of a life.

This has become such a cliché that even the people who say it are probably not quite sure what they mean, or what kind of dark monster we might have produced. But it is still doled out regularly as consolation.

'I usually tell the patients that about 70 per cent of miscarried babies would have been handicapped in some way,' says a Northern family doctor. 'Perhaps it is rather a high estimate, but it cheers them up.'

In fact, it has been estimated that 50 per cent of all conceptions in normal people are chromosomally abnormal and that of all babies who are miscarried in the first twelve weeks, 60 per cent have provable chromosomal abnormalities.

These abnormalities account for children with Down's Syndrome (mongolism) and various types of mental and physical handicap.

The age factor

As a woman gets older, there is more chance of a chromosomal error called a trisomy where one extra chromosome is present in each cell. Seventy-five per cent of Down's Syndrome babies are miscarried and 95 per cent of babies with Turner's Syndrome, the sex chromosome abnormality which means that a child who is a girl is genetically a male.

The older the woman, the more likely she is to miscarry and she has a bigger chance of miscarrying a chromosomally abnormal child. Usually, a chromosomal abnormality is just a 'bad luck' event, but if it occurs more than once it is possible that the doctor will recommend you to see a geneticist.

Balanced translocation

If you have a balanced translocation problem and are sent to see a genetics councillor, it means that each of the parent's sex cells contains the right amount of chromosomal material but some are permanently in the wrong place so that he or she produces an unusually high proportion of abnormal ova or sperm.

This could mean that the chances of having a normal child are considerably lowered.

The geneticist will translate the complicated facts for you and work out your chances of a normal child. Each case is different and you may still have the chance of a normal pregnancy. This kind of problem only happens in about 5 per cent of couples.

DIANNE and her husband were trying for another pregnancy after she had had six miscarriages. Their appointment with a gynaecologist was devastating. 'He was busy. We had to wait an hour and a half to see him. Then he just came out with the terrible news. "There's something wrong with you genetically. You'll probably never have another child and if you do it will be deformed." ' Dianne cried. But their appointment with a geneticist went well. 'He was wonderful. He told me I had a balanced translocation of the chromosomes and a fifty–fifty chance of a normal baby. We decided to go ahead.' Dianne became pregnant again and an amniocentesis test told them that the foetus was unlikely to have spina bifida or Down's Syndrome.

This test extracts some of the amniotic fluid to screen it for such defects and is normally done at sixteen weeks.

She now has a healthy child, Marianne, aged fifteen months. 'We nearly gave up when the first doctor was so depressing. Now I am so glad we chanced it.'

Could there have been anything else wrong?

Some of the most hideous handicaps possible can occur in a growing baby. No matter how much a miscarriage upsets you, you have to be thankful that you did not have a pregnancy which would have resulted in a child with any of these defects: some babies who are miscarried have been found to have conditions such as anencephaly – a foetus without a brain; exomphalos – the baby has no wall to its abdomen and the intestines protrude through the uterus. More commonly, the foetus may have spina bifida, in which his spinal cord has not developed properly. These are called neural tube defects and happen in about 5 per cent of miscarriages.

Is it all in the mind?

Does a woman's psychological attitude have any effect on whether or not she miscarries?

Dr H. Michel-Wolfromm, a psychologist who organized a survey of 60 women who had had recurrent miscarriages found that emotional factors played a part in about 20 per cent of cases.[6]

Thirty-three of them didn't get on well with their husbands. Forty-four women had a 'poor maternal urge' – they declared they desperately wanted a child, but Michel-Wolfromm decided that they didn't really want a baby.

Is it because I'm immune to my husband?

This is the big breakthrough area of research. It has now been found that many women who miscarry are physically rejecting the foetus in the same way that the body rejects a transplanted organ. It is now possible to be immunized against this possibility (see Chapter 14).

So many things can go wrong in early pregnancy that it is a wonder anyone ever gets a baby at all – a miracle that any child ever struggles through those vital first three months!

CHAPTER 6

The women who hope

'I am angry. I have had fourteen miscarriages and so many of them were ignored and never investigated by doctors. It's such a waste of life. One of those babies might have been a Prime Minister.' JOANNA, 38, married to a postman.

Some women who miscarry become obsessional in their endless longing for a child. It can lead to deep depression and, in some cases, marriage casualties.

'If someone said to me, "Jump over that cliff and there's a baby for you," I would jump. I would do *anything*.' TRACEY, 26, cosmetics saleswoman.

'After the miscarriage I just sat there, only getting up to see to the family if I absolutely had to. My husband, normally understanding, finally blew his top. The experience nearly wrecked our marriage.' LIZ, wife of a stockbroker.

The depression which sometimes follows miscarriage can have a disastrous effect on a marriage. For the lucky, strong partnerships, the trauma is temporary. For others it can cause marriage breakdown.

JOANNA is beautiful, with big brown eyes, short, cropped, blonde hair. She enjoys a party, perhaps a drink, a laugh

... Men fall for her instantly. 'The crazy thing is that I didn't want children in the first place. My first pregnancy was an accident. When I lost it I felt a bit sad but philosophical.' Her first husband was an experimental engineer in a car factory.

'He was a bit possessive, didn't like me to work, so after the first couple of years I stayed at home and we started to try for a baby again. I had a miscarriage for the second time at about 12 weeks.

'I couldn't understand afterwards why I felt so terrible. Depression seemed to take over.

'I couldn't stand to be in a room with more than two people. Once, only my grandmother and my parents were sitting there but I had to go and sit in the garden. I couldn't go back until they had all gone home.'

At first, she didn't see any connection with these strange feelings and the miscarriages she had recently undergone.

'I had never been a mothering kind of person. Babies always screamed when they looked at me. I wouldn't go near them. My sister had babies when I was living at home. I don't remember even giving them a bottle or changing a nappy. I was more interested when they grew older and got to the toddler stage. I could talk more easily to them and show them things. But I wasn't keen on babies.'

Slowly, she began to connect her depression with the miscarriages. 'I felt so strange. I would go into a sort of trance when I was out of touch with reality. We owned three dogs, yet I said to my husband, "When are you going to buy us a dog?" '

For twelve years Joanna kept trying for a baby.

'It fell into a pattern. For five or six months of the year, I would be OK, buy clothes, have a good time, buy a dog, build a duck pond . . . you name it! Every summer I got pregnant. Every autumn I would lose it. I was normally in deep depression by Christmas. Christmas, of course, made it worse. For those five or six months I would be in what I can only call total darkness. Life passed me by. I seemed to sit in a corner. That was all. I don't even remember cooking. My husband became a good cook which was just as well.

'The doctor sent me to a psychiatrist who never mentioned the miscarriage and didn't seem to connect them in any way with my feelings. They also arranged that I should go to a day centre. I was collected by bus every day and taken there. I sat there all day, then they brought me home and I sat in the corner at home. The psychiatrist gave me drugs. I was offered ECT (electro-convulsive therapy) but I refused it. My sister had been given it and it affected her memory.

'Why did I plod on trying for a baby? I was afraid not to. I couldn't face the alternatives. It was silly, because I had jobs when I wanted to work. I could have had a good career and, with my first husband, we wanted for nothing. I could have had a good life without children, but I just couldn't face it. Once, I said to a deacon at church, "How can I thank God for eternal life when I can't even face tomorrow?" '

Her husband did not seem very upset when she miscarried. 'If I announced that we would have a baby in so many months' time he would say, "Great!" but I don't think he ever thought of them as babies. He would be disappointed but that was as far as it went. He hadn't actually lost anything. Life carried on as normal for him. He would comfort me when I cried, when I did some of the stupid things I did.

After twelve miscarriages, I came home terribly unhappy because I had asked the hospital to sterilize me and they had refused on the grounds that I wasn't in a fit state to consent. In the middle of the night, I came downstairs and took an overdose, anything I could find. I went a bit O.T.T. and took pain-killers and anti-depressants, the lot. Something must have woken up my husband – possibly the dog, who was barking as I had shut him out – and he called the ambulance. When I came home, I just lay in bed for a week. I couldn't get up. Eventually I asked him, "Why did you call an ambulance?" He looked at me. "I thought about it," he said.

'It made me think! You see, by that time he had had enough. I was so busy always with trying to conceive, too involved with losing the babies to try very much to be anything for him. I was too unstable for it to work.

'I would be normal sometimes. We went to a dinner and I was sitting next to a couple who were old friends. The wife told me she was expecting again. I congratulated them and was fine. I was really pleased for her. "Isn't it wonderful," I said. "They are having a baby." But during the second course I burst into tears and spent the rest of the evening in the loo, crying.

'After we split up I started to get interested in, of all things, rabbit breeding as a hobby. One of the chaps I knew through it phoned and invited me for Christmas. "Don't be miserable at Christmas," he said. "Come and spend it with me and the wife."

'Through them I met his wife's brother, John. A "Teddy-boy" with long sideburns and winkle-pickers, even an ear-ring in his ear. My mother nearly had a fit! He was working as a postman. Within a week we were in love and incredibly happy. One minute I was in the pub with my friends, saying to Sheila in the ladies: "I do like your brother." The next minute he was ringing up to say he'd found me a flat.

'He telephoned me on New Year's Eve to say he had found it, fetched me on New Year's Day and that was it. He was 29. I was 33. I worried in case I wouldn't be able to have a baby by him. I started marking up the calendar with the 'right' days: Early night! Don't stay out late tonight! Don't work too hard! He already had a child by a previous marriage so I thought well, at least he is all right.

'As my mother had feared, it meant a drop in life style to manage on a postman's wage, but I never minded.'

Joanna and her husband live in a basement flat now, near a railway.

She found her new man was not as sympathetic over her depressions as her first husband. 'He didn't know how to cope when I was down. He soon loses patience with me, which is surprising as normally he is a very patient man.'

While she was having so many miscarriages Joanna and her husband had been given chromosome tests which proved normal and hormone tablets which failed to maintain a twelfth pregnancy.

After her second marriage, she moved to a new area and new hospital. She had a hysterosalpingogram (an X-ray test which involves introducing a dye into the uterus and Fallopian tubes). It was found that she had a bi-cornate uterus. The consultant at her local hospital referred her to a more experienced surgeon at a London Teaching Hospital. She had an operation known as a Tonkins Vieroplasty in London and a few months later was given the all-clear to start trying for a pregnancy. But still no luck, so a further laparoscopy was done – which revealed that her tubes were blocked. She was booked for corrective surgery but in the meantime changed her mind.

'I had a dream in which I could feel everything associated with the operation. When I woke up I said immediately, "I'm not having that operation."

'John and I went for a walk. I told him that I had accepted the real possibility of childlessness now and I could cope with it. I was then 36.

'That week my period didn't come. I went to the pharmacy and bought a pregnancy testing kit, which I did the minute John had left the house for church. I couldn't wait for him to go. I nearly pushed him out of the house. Then I did the test and went to meet him after the service.

'They were all having coffee in the vestry. I whispered to John, "Don't say anything, but I'm pregnant." But he shouted at the top of his voice, "She's pregnant!" '

Joanna finally had a baby – David – when she was 37.

'I know I was obsessional. But at least I know now that I am normal. I can have children. During those years of trying I felt such a freak, such a "weirdo". I felt that women were built to have children and I had failed. When I finally had a baby, after all that, I felt very peculiar. He was in special care for fourteen days. I felt he wasn't mine.

'In the end they were having to come and get me to feed him when he woke up. I struggled to feed him but he wouldn't latch on. He was screaming with hunger and I was crying because I couldn't feed him. When we met, we were both in tears!

'On the fourteenth day the nurse said, "You can have him with you now." I was so frightened, I didn't really want him. I said to her, "No, you keep him a bit longer. I don't think he is ready to come out of the incubator." But they insisted and pushed him into my arms.

'I held him. There was a mirror above the sink and I suddenly saw us both standing there. Me with a baby in my arms. I just couldn't believe it was me.

'After that we were both totally happy; some of the best moments are during the midnight feed. David will fall asleep in my arms and look so helpless.

I cry every time.

'Looking back, I wish they had paid more attention to my early miscarriages. If they couldn't save that particular miscarriage they could be kind and say, "If we can't save this one, we'll try to find out what went wrong."

'After all, all life is precious and enough money is spent on abortion. My last consultant said, "It's disgraceful, the way you've been treated. There is no need for you to go through all this."

'If only I had met him years ago, I might have a son of twenty now. It's all been such a waste.'

Why does a woman who miscarries go on and on trying for a baby?

It is not unusual for a woman who has miscarried once to go on trying for a child until she has had ten, twelve – even fifteen miscarriages. Some psychologists see this as something which has become obsessional.

'The odd thing is that she may not even have wanted a child particularly in the first instance – but once she has miscarried, it becomes a challenge. She will keep on trying to become pregnant.

'She will see herself in a rose-coloured romantic dream of motherhood which, if she finally succeeds, may disappoint her,' says research psychologist Kenneth Gannon. 'If she finally gives birth she may panic because the reality does not live up to her romance. So she may be horrified at the practical prospect of feeding and nappy changing, and may even reject the child, which she has wanted for so long.' He is anxious for further research to be done on this aspect of miscarriage. 'Long-term medical studies are desperately needed.'

'Before my miscarriage my husband was kind and understanding. Afterwards he accused me of not looking after our children properly . . . it nearly wrecked our marriage.'

Until her miscarriage, LIZ and her husband, stockbroker Derek, had everything they wanted: a comfortable house in the home countries; two children, aged three and a half and eighteen months. Money was no real problem.

'Everything was fine until I discovered I was pregnant again. A bit of a shock at first, but we soon got over it and found ourselves cheerfully making plans. Just like the first time.'

A professional nursery nurse before her marriage, Liz loves children. At eight weeks, however, bleeding started. 'I was too busy to notice it at first. My daughter had been awake all night with earache and I had to ring the doctor for her. By afternoon, though, the bleeding had changed to red. I phoned the doctor on call who gave me the usual advice: Go to bed and rest.'

Liz suddenly realized how much she wanted this unplanned pregnancy. 'I wanted this baby as much as I had wanted the previous ones. I lay in bed, willing my contracting womb to calm down and hold on. I rang the surgery again and this time a doctor came round. She explained that my cervix was open. She was kind, patient, sympathetic – everything I could have wished for. I didn't want to go into hospital, so she suggested I phoned the surgery if

things became beyond my control. But two days later, with increasing pain, I had to go to hospital, where I was examined by a wonderful woman doctor, a senior house officer in Gynaecology. She decided to wait for four hours before deciding what to do. By the time she returned to me I was bleeding heavily, so a D and C was decided upon.

'I was lucky. They fitted me into a cancellation in the operating theatre, leaving me just enough time to phone my husband, who was allowed to be with me. He was the first face I saw when I came round.

'Medically, I have no cause for complaint. The medical staff were marvellous. But when I got home, depression hit me. The first few days were a blur. I had never known such pain and anguish.

'All day I would sit there, dragging myself up to get the children's meals only when it became absolutely essential. I would be on the phone for hours, desperately wanting to talk about it. People told me I was lucky. I had two beautiful children already.

'That made me worse. I thought my children were OK. They had people caring for them already. What about my baby? Who would look after him? My husband who had always been so kind and caring, now started to tell me to pull myself together. He came home one evening and my little boy was running around in the garden, wearing only his vest. He blew his top with me, said he felt scared to leave me alone with the children.

'What was the matter with me? Why couldn't I take care of them? He broke down in tears in the end. I felt he had abandoned me – let me down when I needed him most!'

Her doctor called in a psychiatrist. 'He really upset me. He started attacking me and asked why did I think I shouldn't have a miscarriage. Other women had them. What was so special about me?

'My husband explained that he had thought of taking me on a holiday to recuperate. The psychiatrist pooh-poohed the idea, saying that a holiday wouldn't help a depressed woman.

'My husband got cross. On the whole the psychiatrist didn't help. I must have gone on feeling like this for about three months . . . until I got pregnant again and miscarried. This time the doctors didn't seem to believe I'd really been pregnant. I had a psychiatric history, you see, now . . .'

For Liz, the good news is that she is once more pregnant. She has passed three months and is happy and hopeful.

Her husband is not so happy. 'He is worried to death. I have never known him so uptight. He is just afraid that I'll get depressed again if things go wrong. It has got to be all right this time.'

'When I knew that it might be my husband's sperm which was stopping me from carrying a child, I even considered going with another man. I would do anything to have a baby.'

TRACEY is 26. Pregnant again. She is living apart from her husband in another town twenty miles away so that she can be eligible to attend a hospital she likes for treatment, rather than one near her home where she had an unpleasant experience of miscarriage.

She lives now at her old home, with her widowed mother. A break-up between her mother and her husband means that they are not on speaking terms, so he is not welcome at the house.

'When he comes to see me at weekends, he parks outside the house and I run into the car to join him for a while. It's not a very happy way of living but it is for the sake of the baby.

Tracey has had two miscarriages. Small, thin faced, her nervous eyes betray her fears for the new pregnancy. 'I don't want to be away from Steve. I didn't intend this to break us up. I just hope I'll get a baby out of this then perhaps we can live together again.

'They say that I am the strong partner of the two. When we married, a friend asked, "Is this going to last a lifetime?" and I replied, "Well, what does these days?" When I had two miscarriages Steve started to blame me for losing the babies. I think that's a bad sign, when you start talking about whose fault it is. I'll never forget what he said. "It's nothing to do with me. It's your fault."

'He didn't go willingly for a sperm count. I had to persuade him.

'The result was a 65 per cent abnormality. It was explained that this means that 65 per cent of the sperm were abnormal and might result in an abnormal foetus if fertilized.

'But I still wanted a baby so I even thought of going with another man. I always said that if that was what I had to do to get a baby I would do it. That sounds awful, but when you get desperate, you'll do anything.

'I didn't go with anyone else, as it happens, and this is Steve's baby, but I'll cope with it on my own if I have to.'

Small and serious, she perches worriedly on the edge of the sofa in her mother's home on a Northern council estate.

'I've coped with lots of things. In a matter of months, I coped with the death of my father, a serious quarrel between my husband and my mother – and two miscarriages.'

Tracey's first miscarriage was at nine weeks and all over in half an hour. 'No pain to speak of and I saw my little "mouse" – that's how I used to visualize it when I was expecting – I saw the little "mouse" floating in a bedpan. The staff put it down to bad luck and said it was "probably for the best".

'I saw the baby and assumed from what I saw in the bedpan that it was a boy, but the nurses said I couldn't possibly be right. I touched it and by the time a middle-aged nurse came back, I wouldn't part with it.

' "Come along, Tracey," she said. "Give it to me." I know it's not a nice thing to think about – floating around in your blood, but when it is yours, you want it. The nurse was kind and put her arm around me.'

Tracey's second miscarriage was much worse. 'I was taken into hospital one evening. I had been bleeding and they insisted on examining me. I pleaded with the woman doctor not to – but she insisted and reckoned everything was all right. I didn't believe her.

'At midnight, I woke up soaked. The waters had broken. Three minutes later I started with the pains and these continued every two and three minutes. The worst thing I've ever been through in my life. Terrible pain. I thought I was dying.

'The nurse couldn't get the doctor to come. He sent her back with what looked like two aspirin tablets. She said, "They'll take about twenty minutes to work." But twenty minutes later, I was still writhing in pain. On a main ward, I didn't want to wake everyone, so I chewed a big hole in the sheet. I was crying, saying, "Oh God", and I hardly had time to say that before I got another pain. I had never had a baby or been to relaxation classes and I just didn't expect the intensity of the pains. They went on for six hours. a nurse changed the sheets but no one sat with me. The only thing anyone told me was that it might have been an incompetent cervix. Later my husband found out that it could have been something abnormal in his sperm.

'I was that shocked and relieved that the pain was over. The nurse said, "Don't go thinking that full-term labour is anything like as bad as that, because it's not."

'Three months later the consultant was persuaded to get my file out and said that the sex of the foetus had not been recorded. I should have asked earlier.

'After I'd been in labour about six and a half hours, the patient opposite me in the ward was quite stroppy when a nurse said, "Good morning." "Is it?" she said. "I've been kept awake all night – by her!" She was trying to keep her baby. I was in shock. I'd just lost mine. The nurse said to her, "Right Mrs So and So. Have you got your cigarettes and lighter?" She took her down to the toilet. I had never smoked and I rarely drink. I had lost my baby when I'd played it really straight all down the line. I left the ward like a zombie.

'At home it was worse for my father who was very ill.

'He had had an operation for cancer and come home. He'd been delighted when I told him I was pregnant. He put it in his diary – "Keep your sights on September."

'Dad had been thrilled to bits. I remember him patting my tummy when I was about fourteen weeks and saying, "That's my grandchild in there." It gave him new hope. After the miscarriage I had to phone up. The doctor was with my dad at the time. My mum tried to tell him but he just cried and cried. He said, "That's it. Everything's just going now. I'm not bothered anymore." He was 58 – a postman, higher grade. He loved his work so much he had helped out with the Christmas rush, then died in the February.

'I blamed my body for not only letting me down but my father as well. He put his arm around me when I saw him after the miscarriage. "Never mind," he said. And this man was dying!'

Now she is pregnant again. As she had difficulty in conceiving, she was put on Clomid, the drug to help her ovulate. 'The GP tried to encourage me. He said, "You're a good age to have a baby. You don't drink or smoke. It will be all right." I got that fed up with being the only one in both our families not to have children. I couldn't accept being childless for life. In the hospital here – the new hospital – they are very, very good and told me that I would have to consider artificial insemination or something like that (AID). That's where the problem starts, because my husband says, "I'm not having anyone else's child." '

Tracey and her husband originally moved back to Tracey's home after her father died. 'It was Steve's idea. He felt my mother would need us with her. That we ought to do it. After about a year, my mum decided she wanted to be on her own again.

'Tempers frayed and now they just don't speak to each other. I'm in the middle of it. Mum goes on about Steve and he goes on about her. I just go from week to week, counting the weeks, hoping this baby will be all right.

'I'm fourteen weeks now, but at the back of my mind I wonder, "Will I reach 16?" I look at all the pregnant ladies. I daren't shop. Last time I bought little knitted things. You get to a stage, though, where you think it's silly to tempt fate. I gave the last lot to my niece. That was bad. She came round one day, not knowing I was here and her baby was wearing my child's suit. I had to sit and smile, which was hard.

'Mum and I went shopping last week. They had some lovely baby suits in a sale. Mum asked me, "Do you want one?" I said, "No. I'd better not!" I think she has bought one and sneaked it upstairs, though I'm not supposed to know.

'I feel bitter when I read the Birth announcements in the paper: "Many thanks to Pontefract General." I feel jealous. "Well, that's fine for you. You've got a healthy baby."

'Hopefully, I'll get a baby out of this. It's the only thing that's getting me through this bad time – the memory of my lost babies and my dad keeps me going.'

CHAPTER 7

The men – is it worth it?

'I had had enough . . . I couldn't bear what it was doing to us. It was ruining our sex lives and making my wife ill. I decided on a vasectomy.'

Recurrent miscarriages are a drain on any couple, with the consequent ill-health of the wife and the routine of 'sex to order' for the husband if they go on trying endlessly for a baby.

ANDY found it all too much for him. He decided he had had enough, partly because he was so upset by the way his wife suffered in miscarriage.

Andy and Chris have a sandstone house in the north of England. Clean stone, thanks to the Clean Air Act which brought light and air to the 'dark satanic mills' of Yorkshire and Lancashire. He is a telephone engineer, passionate about his hobby of running a magazine for new writers. With curly hair and a moustache, he is affable and fun – only his fidgeting hands reveal that Andy worries a lot. He has certainly worried about his wife.

They had been married a few years when, finding themselves equipped with all modern conveniences – a newly restored house, video, microwave, etc., they decided to go in for a baby.

For nearly a year, no luck. They were on the verge of making an appointment to see the doctor when Chris conceived. But she soon became ill with constant sickness.

Chris had been a nursery nurse. She wears large specs, has long loose limbs, lots of charm and is essentially very nice. During the pregnancy she couldn't eat anything at all, she was so sick. 'The doctor didn't seem interested,' says Chris. 'He told me on the phone that I had morning sickness and he seemed to think I was exaggerating. Eventually he asked, "Do you really want this baby?" ' In the end Andy took her to the doctor himself, wrapped in a blanket. 'I had to carry her. She was so weak. We were living in a nightmare of buckets, with her permanently so sick. Within half an hour she was in hospital on a drip. At last, they were taking it seriously.'

After a pregnancy in which Chris was never really well, their son Sam was born, but he too seemed ill. He was losing weight rapidly and didn't seem to digest his food. 'We thought there was something wrong with him and kept asking the doctor about it but he said, "No, he's just a colicky baby." ' At nine weeks, he was very ill and the doctor found out that he had a problem with a muscle at the base of his stomach. It was too tight and wouldn't allow food through. So, at nine weeks, he had to have an operation.

'The worst thing for us was seeing that tiny figure wheeled away on an enormous trolley.'

They soon began to try for another baby. Chris became pregnant quickly but the sickness problem began. 'We never went anywhere without the sick bucket,' says Andy. 'Have bucket, will travel! The house was littered with piles of wet tissues. She had begun to bleed but, as she had experienced some bleeding during the first pregnancy we thought nothing of it.' Two days after the bleeding started, Andy went out for a drink. 'It was the first time I had been out for a drink for ages. When I returned she wasn't there. My father-in-law was at home looking after Sam. I went straight up to the hospital.' He was greatly upset when he saw his wife. 'She was in Casualty still. The baby seemed to be dripping out of her. The stench was horrific. I can't describe how I felt. I was devastated. It was like a death.

'I had imagined how we would be as a family. I had taken the lads at work out for a drink to celebrate. I always think of him or her as a person. It was alive and it died. Afterwards it was awful at the hospital for Chris. They made her have breakfast with the other patients. Women who were pregnant were sitting there. She just broke down and cried.'

Chris remembers: 'I told him to go out that night. At ten o'clock I stood up and thought I'd make a cup of coffee. Then suddenly, I had such a pain. I thought, "Something's not right here." Over the phone the doctor said, "It sounds as though you have had a miscarriage." He said he would be with me in twenty minutes. In fact, he was a lot quicker than that. He examined me and said, "That's it." The placenta was coming away in broken-up pieces, like liver.

'My mum came with me in the ambulance. It was very painful and they gave me some pethidine. I was so cold. My main feeling was fear . . . having the anaesthetic I felt so frightened of the operation that it overrode everything. It all happened so quickly. At ten I was at home; at 12.15 I was in the theatre. There was no time for pre-meds. I had never had an operation before.

'They went through the rigmarole of making sure I had actually lost it, though my doctor had known at home. It was obvious. When I came round I felt awful and didn't sleep for the rest of the night. One minute I was having a baby. The next minute I wasn't. Was it all a dream? Would I wake up and find that everything was all right? When I cried at the breakfast table the next day a nurse put her arm round me and asked, "What's the matter? Is it what has happened?" My main worry was *why* it had happened. I started to remember that I hadn't been so sick with this pregnancy as I was the first time. Obviously this was because it hadn't been developing properly. It wasn't putting the same demands on my body. It would have been better for the baby if I had been sick. I felt shocked. At first I reacted quite well. I was a bit quiet. It took about a fortnight to sink in. After that came the decision. What are we going to do? Are we going to have some more? If we do, can it happen again? I can't go through that again.

'All these thoughts . . . the medics' attitude is, "Go on. Have another. You'll be all right."

'Before we decided, I went into this sickness problem. It had apparently been caused originally by hypo-glycaemia – low blood sugar levels – so I had glucose tolerance tests and the results were OK. The level was all right.'

Eventually Andy decided to have 'the snip'. 'A vasectomy seemed the answer. We were only in our twenties and all the baby business seemed to be robbing us of our lives. Now we are over thirty but while we are having babies, miscar-rying etc., we are completely robbed of all fun in life. Sex went out of the window – our sex life was abandoned because whenever she thought of sex she thought of babies and the misery she had with them.'

Chris says: 'Andy left the decision to me because, after all, it's my body. I have to be sick and go through it. It took a few weeks but as soon as we had come to the decision I knew it was right. I am certain that for us it is wrong to have any more. Not just for me but what about Andy having to look after me while I'm sick or in hospital?

'We are lucky to have Sam. As for our relationship, we are closer. Nobody else could or would understand because they're never been through it. They didn't know what to say to us and even now close friends are not as close as they were. After all, they've gone on to have second babies and we haven't.

'I was saying the other day, "I wonder why they haven't been," and I'm sure some friends don't come to see us because of the baby situation. They feel they can't talk about their babies. Up to a few months ago I would have been jealous. I would watch friends. If they already had a girl I would think, "If they have a boy I shall be very upset. Why can they have one of each and I can't?"

'I think we made the right decision for Sam, too. He's a nice little lad, but he is a handful. We've got one child and we'll look after him as best we can. Not spoil him, but give him as much as we can.'

Although they have made their deci-sion and Andy has had the vasectomy, they still get pressure from the family to have another child. 'Our parents were quite good. They said, "What about *your* lives?"

'But sometimes they say things such as, "Get on and have another," or, "If you have another one!" I say, "We are not going to have another. We have come to a decision." '

Says Chris: 'Andy reacts differently to me. I'm very emotional but that doesn't mean he didn't care as much. I was always bursting into tears after the baby. He would just go quiet, twiddle his fingers and pick his nails.'

Says Andy: 'At work after the baby it was awful. I'd been celebrating only the week before. Now I was upset about los-ing the baby and a lot of my mates had wives getting pregnant. I just muddled along. Now we've made the decision we feel better. As it was, I was worried to death if she was only two days late.'

Chris admits she sometimes feels, '. . . a bit of a failure. But I try to brush it off and think of other things. I feel like cud-dling Sam all the time.' She has recently taken up a new interest. She makes dolls and sells them at a weekly market.

'I got to the stage where I never refused an invitation, an opportunity to stay out of the house. Being on shift work, it was easy for me to go to the pub to do the crossword with a colleague, perhaps stay a bit longer, have another beer . . .

'It's an escape route, I suppose.' JOHN is a physicist at the UK nuclear plant at Sellafield.

Four years ago he held his dead, still-born, baby daughter in his arms. At 26 weeks, it was the worst of his wife's seventeen miscarriages. He will never forget it.

He says, 'It was a year of hell. First my father died, then I was busy with a court case for the firm when I got an urgent message.

'My wife was losing the baby. And we had really thought that this time, having passed the first three months, we were really going to be lucky.'

Summoned to his wife Lorraine, John had to get her to hospital where she was given a drug to halt the contractions. 'It was magic and everything stopped. But after a few days the doctors had to stop giving her the drug for fear of side-effects.

'She went into labour as soon as it was stopped so the doctors planned to get her to a hospital 120 miles away where there was a good intensive care unit for the baby. It was quite exciting. Ambulance and police escort dashed along. Lights flashing, sirens wailing – Lorraine on a drip with a special medical team at her side – I was tearing along behind trying to keep up!

'The obstetricians were great. They really thought the baby might be all right. Only the midwife seemed doubtful.'

Sadly, the baby was born dead. 'Then we went home and it was Christmas which made it seem worse, somehow . . .'

John and Lorraine are examples of the stress caused by recurrent miscarriage. 'I've had so many miscarriages that it has become a way of life. In the end it upset John so much he started staying out late and took to drink. In the end he developed a real alcoholism problem.'

LORRAINE is active, outgoing, with a house full of animals and the two children she has fostered with a view to adoption. At 36, she has had seventeen miscarriages.

'I'm a village girl. Everyone knows me and has always known me for the animals, the horses, dogs and cats I keep. When I kept miscarrying the whole village seemed to know the answer. Women would stop me in the street and tell me to stop messing about with pets and give John the children he wanted. We both took a lot of flak.

'In the end we started blaming each other, particularly when we were trying to adopt and felt we were under scrutiny. Drink was John's reaction to all the worry but now, thank goodness, he has conquered the problem.'

Lorraine's miscarriages varied from eight weeks to 26.

She sought help everywhere, but even the top men of the medical profession couldn't tell them why she miscarried or provide a successful treatment. 'We travelled all over the place, to hospitals, even to professors, but there was just no solution. We thought immunotherapy might be the answer, but it was not suitable in our case.'

Lorraine and John live near the nuclear plant of Sellafield. Lorraine was born in Seascale, the village where many of the children contracted leukaemia. 'But I don't think miscarriages were ever linked with that,' says Lorraine. 'I don't think there was a specially high number in Seascale.'

Their hardest time was in 1985 when a pregnancy went to nearly 27 weeks and their little girl was born dead. 'It was hell for John. He sat up all night holding her body. The hospital staff said that although it wasn't technically a still-birth which it would have been at 28 weeks, I could still have a funeral. They strongly advised me against it, as they thought it would upset me too much. I shall always regret that I didn't have one. John and I have so little to remember of Nia Helen.

'We called her Nia because it is an old Welsh name and John has Welsh ancestry. We didn't even have a photograph.

'I was too muzzy at the time to make any decision. She was born in the early hours of the morning and I was released from hospital that same morning. I would have liked some counselling, but there was nothing. We held a little family memorial service but that was all.'

Finding village life intolerable after all the miscarriages, they moved to a new housing estate. 'That was a mistake. All the young couples were moving in and, of course, having babies. It was the main topic of conversation. Coffee mornings, with baby chat, appeals for playgroup funds . . . it was babies, babies, babies and I couldn't stand it.

'I felt that women after miscarriage are treated very badly and I was campaigning very hard to help them to get better treatment. I worked with a very close friend, Lindy.

'She was 34 and had eight miscarriages but doctors had advised her to stop trying as she had a blood condition.

'I presumed she had stopped, but one day she was rushed to hospital after a miscarriage and given a D and C. It seemed she hadn't told anyone and was well into a pregnancy. She hadn't even told her husband.

'She came home suddenly and haemorrhaged. The doctors couldn't stop it and she died.

'I was absolutely shattered. She was full of fun, a joke a minute, and very attractive! I remembered that I had seen her knitting baby clothes but I had assumed they were for other people as she'd told me she wasn't trying for a baby any more. When we went through her things we found sacks and sacks of knitted baby clothes. She had never really given up.'

Lorraine began to feel that miscarriages could 'take over' her life. 'I met a woman who had devoted her home to preparation for a baby. It was spotless, decorated twice a year. A nursery was ready. A new pram stood waiting. But she kept having miscarriages. The house reeked of boredom.

'I decided I just could not let myself get like that. John helped me by buying a dog to breed from. We moved house and set up kennels and an animal rescue centre. I got interested in breeding. I show at Crufts and other places. John comes with me to drive them around and we've got really interested in it.

'We were finally accepted for fostering, with a view to adoption and now have a boy and a girl, brother and sister aged five and six. We have also said we will take an entire problem family if necessary.

'I have filled my life with other things. But I never stop trying for a baby. I caught myself the other day looking at the calendar and working out the date for intercourse. It has become a way of life and I can't stop.

'My life is now full, so I could face a childless future. People tell me I might get pregnant again now that I have fostered! I only think of babies sometimes now. I was made a judge at Crufts and I was standing in the show ring when it struck me: "Is this what I really want?" '

John has overcome his tendency to drink too much but feels it was a symptom of their shared disappointment about not having children.

'My friends found it difficult to talk about the miscarriages. They would come for a drink and we would talk about everything under the sun except the problem on my mind – the babies.

'It could be because some men feel ashamed if their wives can't have children. I never did. After all, I'd had checks. My sperm count was OK, so we knew there was nothing wrong with us. Why should we feel ashamed?

'The first miscarriages weren't so bad. Just hard luck, we thought, and we were quite optimistic. Then it happened over and over again, but the doctors could find nothing wrong. If only they had, we would have identified the problem.

'The trouble is, the worry is in the house all the time. You can't enjoy the benefits of the freedom of being childless.

'Every time we booked a holiday abroad, Lorraine would be in hospital again . . . or pregnant again . . . so we never in fact got away on holiday for ten years!

'When we were being assessed for adoption we would find ourselves arguing. We would argue about all sorts of things when what we were really arguing about was the baby problem.

'We began to feel we were social outcasts. Most of our friends were having children. Relations seemed to talk about their children, undress their babies in front of Lorraine . . . ask her to hold them. Probably it was unintentional, but it hurt.

'I never minded the trying for a baby. Being of a scientific mind, I quite enjoyed working out ovulation charts, but Lorraine hated it. In the end we said, "Forget it. If it happens, it happens, but we won't let it ruin our lives." '

The fostering of the two children has meant a great deal, plus the shared interest they both have in the dogs.

John's drinking problem is a thing of the past and they both look forward to the day when they can adopt their foster children.

After a miscarriage, husbands are often accused by their wives of not caring enough. Often this is because men are embarrassed about any display of emotion, whereas a woman feels free to cry. A man's suffering can be just as acute.

IAN, who is a cashier, has always been a quiet worrier, given to bottling up his feelings. Starting a family was fraught with problems from the outset, as his wife Margaret found it difficult to conceive. Initially, it took three years for her to become pregnant and she lost the baby at eight weeks. Her doctor explained to her that the baby had died in the womb.

'That was my blackest time,' says Margaret. 'I realized that I was not only going to have trouble conceiving but would have trouble in carrying a baby as well.

'We went on holiday that August. My period was due while we were away but it didn't come. I couldn't wait to get back home to go to the doctor. The result came back positive. I was six weeks pregnant. Ian was delighted. I will never forget the look on his face when I told him. We had a really happy weekend.

'But when I got up for work on Monday some spotting started. I was admitted to hospital straightaway and the bleeding stopped. They kept me in for two weeks then sent me home with instructions to rest. No work.

'Everything went well for the next three months. I was now on hormone tablets three times a day. I had a blood test for spina bifida. Then a scan suggested that my dates were wrong and that I wasn't as far on as I thought. They then insisted on doing another spina bifida test as they felt the first had been done too soon.

'Finally my world collapsed with a phone call to say that my test was a borderline result and would I come in and have it done yet again.

'I phoned the following week for the result and was told that this time it was even higher than before. It looked as if my baby had spina bifida. I had to have

an amniocentesis test (see Chapter 14) just to check this and wait two days for the result.

'How we got through those days I will never know. Then a phone call on the Friday afternoon said the baby was OK. What a Christmas we had!!'

But that was not the end of the problem. January brought a call from the hospital saying that she was to have another scan as she had a placenta praevia. The placenta had slipped its moorings and was lying low in the womb.

'I woke in the night with the pain and bleeding and was whisked back to hospital. I was exactly 28 weeks' pregnant. The young doctor who admitted me said that if the bleeding didn't stop they would have to deliver the baby and since it was very small it didn't have a great chance of survival.'

Margaret admits to being 'nearly hysterical' by this time. Ian was worried, too, and it was around this time that he began to notice that he was losing his hair in small circumscribed patches, about the size of a ten-penny piece.

Margaret stayed in hospital for ten weeks as scans showed that the placenta had settled right over the neck of the womb. Doctors managed to get her to 38 weeks, which was their goal, and her daughter Lauren was delivered by Caesarean section. She weighed 5lbs 3 ounces (2.3 kg).

By this time Ian, aged 31, had lost all his hair. Doctors diagnosed alopecia totalis and put it down to the stress of the worry over Lauren.

Ian – 'I've always been the worrying type' – says that Lauren was worth it! But his hair has never returned in the nine years since she was born, during which time Margaret has had two more healthy children and another miscarriage. 'I needed the hormone tablets to maintain that pregnancy but the doctors wouldn't give me a prescription early enough. Will they never learn!' says Margaret. 'My own doctor offered me sterilization the day I left hosptal and was amazed that I wouldn't take it!'

Some men may not show their own sadness about a miscarriage because they are afraid of upsetting their wives. When she lost a baby at nineteen weeks, EMMA didn't think her husband seemed particularly bothered about it. But she was lucky enough to have a helpful hospital chaplain who arranged a burial, although the baby was well below the 28 week still-birth rule.

EMMA was surprised and pleased that her husband visited the grave nearly every day, finding that it helped him to grieve.

When ANN lost two pregnancies she felt that her husband Leslie was mainly concerned about her. They were both young, in their twenties, and very much in love.

'I just wanted to be around to comfort her,' says Leslie, who works as a head gardener. 'At work my colleagues welcomed me back and seemed to think I would be glad to be back at work and get out of the house and the upset. It wasn't like that at all. I wanted to be with my wife.'

Says Ann: 'My mother had bought a pram for us and was keeping it in her back room.

'She told me that when Leslie went to see her he was ages looking at it and there were tears in his eyes when he came out. He said to her, "Don't worry, mum, We'll fill it for you one day."

'So I knew then how much he cared about it.'

CHAPTER 8

The hospital stay . . . and after

'The way I was treated in hospital was appalling. The depression it caused went on for years and nearly wrecked my family.' CHRISTINE blames her miscarriage and stay in hospital for 'four years of misery'.

It is now seventeen years since the miscarriage. For four years afterwards, she says, her husband had to keep calling in when he should have been working. 'He was terrified I couldn't take care of the children. Just as well. There were times when I could have thrown them across the room.'

Christine feels that the hospital's attitude caused her depression. 'No one talked to me about what had happened. Their feeling seemed to be, "You've had a miscarriage. So what?" I was shell-shocked when I left the hospital and as soon as I got home the misery started.'

As Christine's experience happened some years ago, hospitals might have been expected to improve since then. ELAINE, however, had a miscarriage recently at ten weeks. She says: 'The consultant was sweet. My own doctor was superb.

'But the staff at the hospital were horrible. They said, "You haven't really lost a baby. It was nothing much at this stage. Why are you making so much fuss?" I was in agony – the doctor explained afterwards that this was because the cervix still has to open even at this early stage. They sent my husband away although he'd driven from work breaking all the speed limits to be with me. They just told him I was making a ridiculous fuss and sent him away.

'I had five hours of excruciating pain, much worse than childbirth, then no one talked to me or told me a thing. I didn't know what they'd done with the dead baby – thrown it in the incinerator, I suppose. Then they wheeled me down the main ward through all the happy mothers holding their new babies. A girl in the next bed was there for an abortion. She asked me, "Are you here to get rid of yours?"

'If I had been able to get off the trolley, I would have dragged her out of bed and knocked her down.'

Research psychologist Kenneth Gannon has been studying the psychological effects of miscarriage. He says, 'The insensitivity of some hospitals is unbelievable. It is only too common for a woman who is there after a miscarriage to find herself next to someone in for a deliberate abortion. I see women who have miscarried years ago who still carry a massive burden of unresolved grief. If no one talks to a woman at the time about her experience she never works through what has happened and the resulting depression can be a handicap for the rest of her life. When a woman talks to me about it, she often starts to cry although it was such a long time ago. There is massive bitterness and anger from women who have miscarried.'

He feels that hospitals could prevent this. 'It is common for them to be sent out of hospital with not a word of explanation or comfort. Surely it would not cost the health services very much to lay on someone who could talk to them for half an hour? Medical people need to understand that these women have suffered a real bereavement. To a doctor it may be a routine event, the loss of a cluster of cells.

'To a woman it is the major loss of a baby she has imagined, dreamed about, made plans for, named. Her "John" or "Emma" is dead and she suffers very real grief.'

If you are terribly upset over a first miscarriage, it may be harder for you to carry another baby. Kenneth Gannon feels that the long-term psychological effects on a woman of one miscarriage can make it harder for her to carry another child to term. 'The anxiety and distress has a follow-on effect and will make her permanently anxious and tense in her next pregnancy, worried that it might happen again. This very anxiety makes her more likely to miscarry a second time.

'Research studies on animals have proved this. We have also found that a woman who is given psychological support and encouragement during her pregnancy is more likely to have a successful outcome. One good idea is to give her weekly scans until the danger time of sixteen weeks has passed. This way she is reassured that the foetus is developing normally in the womb.'

He also calls for more attention to be paid to the husband when a woman miscarries. 'Too often, a husband is ignored. He feels left out while his wife battles on to have a baby. As a woman often feels a sense of failure – of not being a proper woman – because she miscarries, men, too, feel that they have failed. A man may also feel guilty when a wife miscarries. A man may remember having intercourse with his wife while she was pregnant. If she lost the baby shortly after that, he will blame himself, wonder whether he has been too rough with her.

'The situation can build up a wall of silence between the couple. They are both "separately" blaming themselves to such an extent that they can't talk about it to each other at all. So marriage problems become inevitable.'

Many women who miscarry are upset that the foetus is just cleared quickly away, out of sight *en route* for the hospital incinerator! Though a stillborn baby (after 28 weeks) is entitled to the ritual of burial. Sometimes with an early miscarriage there is nothing to see, anyway, except clots of blood.

It is understandable that hospitals have to draw the line somewhere, otherwise they would find themselves conducting burial services for the menstrual flow! Some more enlightened hospitals, in fact, have a 'grey area' where a foetus may be buried below that 28 weeks' requirement. TRISHA, who lost her baby at 21 weeks, was delighted that the hospital was prepared to bend the rules. 'They took a photograph of the baby and they buried her. It really made all the difference and we have something to remember of her.'

But are hospitals blamed unfairly for failing to help women who miscarry? At the Queen Elizabeth Hospital, Birmingham, Dr Joe Jordan is Consultant Gynaecologist and Obstetrician. He says, 'It is a question of communication. Often I feel I've explained things carefully to a couple, but they forget what I've said and may declare afterwards that they have been told nothing at all. They may complain that staff in a scan room did not tell them anything. But that is a definite rule. I do not want a patient to discuss her case with other people in the hospital, be it the scan technician or the ward cleaner.

'She should receive information only from the person who can give it her correctly – the doctor – otherwise there would be endless confusion.'

But should it happen that a woman is treated so insensitively? JANE, for instance, complained: 'The foetus I had saved to show the doctor was pushed into a test tube and labelled "Products of Conception" and whisked away in front of me.'

Says Dr Jordan: 'Of course this sort of thing shouldn't happen and I would be very angry if one of my staff behaved like that. But insensitive things will happen in a big organization, which the hospital is. Many people are involved and they don't always behave as one would wish. There is also a feeling in such a vast organization that "someone else" has done things – so there can be omissions!'

Dr Jordan also feels that anger and bitterness are a natural part of the woman's feelings over her miscarriage. 'It has happened and it is impossible for anyone to tell her why. She is angry about the blow fate has dealt her and a natural feeling is to turn that anger on to the doctor. Facilities are available to help a woman cope with miscarriage.

'In this hospital, for instance, a social worker is always on hand to come to talk with her. But perhaps patients don't realize that she is there if required. Perhaps we can learn what women need – a list of practical do's and don'ts after miscarriage could be provided. If this is what patients need then we'll be happy to provide one.'

CHRISTINE feels that she never 'worked through' her feelings of despair over her miscarriage. Tiny, five foot two, she is now dwarfed by her three children. The men of the family are six-footers, including her husband. She miscarried with her first child at eleven weeks. She telephoned the emergency service deputizing for her GP because it was Saturday night. 'An Asian doctor came out to me. He did not seem to speak any English. He gave me a very rough internal, then apparently panicked. I was bleeding all over the shop! He sent for an ambulance. I had thought I was booked into one hospital but this ambulance took me to another, an inner city hospital where all the notices are in Urdu and Gujarati.

'The nurse sent Bob away and I was

left on a trolley in a corridor for three hours – eight o'clock until 11 p.m. – because the staff were busy and I suppose we should know better than to bother a busy casualty department on a Saturday night! Eventually, they came and had a look at me, another poke and a prod and said, "Yes, it's a miscarriage. We're keeping you in but there's no need for a D and C. Tell them when you get to the ward that there's no need for you to go to theatre."

'On the ward the Night Sister wouldn't believe me – or the porter – when we tried to give our message. So they got me ready for theatre even though I wouldn't be going until the next day. I was rather het up so the nurse said she would fetch a cup of tea and a sleeping pill. An hour later neither had arrived and someone said, "Oh sorry, we've given them to the wrong person." They wouldn't let me have another pill. "We've signed that one out." So I never got my sleeping pill or my tea.

'I didn't sleep all night. My blood pressure was apparently sky high. I lay awake panicking.

'In the morning the girl in the next bed was a sixteen year old having an abortion. The next day the doctor came round at 10 a.m. and asked, "Why is this patient ready for theatre?" He was very angry with them for ignoring his message. When they explained, he was quite sympathetic to me. He said, "You've had nothing to eat. Would you like something?" I said, "I'd like a wash, a cup of tea and a slice of bread and jam!"

'I was shell-shocked when I left the hospital. I'd had the feeling throughout that their attitude was: "You've had a miscarriage, so what?" The depression set in when I got home and everyone was busy talking about everything else. At work, they'd obviously decided to pretend that nothing had happened. There was only one colleague who came round and said, "I didn't know what to say, but I'm here." That helped.

'Some people told me I would feel better when I had another baby. A year later I had Robert and I thought the depression would lift but it didn't. It got worse . . . and worse.

'In those days (1972) people didn't talk about things like post-natal depression and certainly not in connection with a miscarriage. I carried on outwardly as normal, went shopping, cooked the meals, coping with things at home, but sometimes I could have thrown the baby across the room. Bob did his best to call home whenever he could escape from his work because he was aware of the state I was in. We were living in an area where there were so many Asians that they didn't speak English at the nearest clinic. Bob worked shifts so could often be at home in the afternoons and I could go out by myself. I think I would have cracked up if that hadn't happened. I wanted to move away from the area, not because I'm a racialist, but because sometimes I was afraid. A West Indian set upon me and threatened me in the street.

'I had another baby, Pauline, but I still felt depressed. I was improving on a superficial level but only because I suppose I buried all my grief.

'In the end we realized we had to move.' Christine believes that it was through her contact with the Miscarriage Association at this stage that she began to 'talk through' her experience.

'I went on a bereavement counselling course – the same people who counselled the victims of the Bradford fire. I have talked about my miscarriage for the first time and it has helped. Bob wouldn't talk about it for ages but we began to discuss it and it brought us together again. I think my third baby Timmy was the result of that. I was not depressed after his birth!'

Christine's husband Bob says he is aware of what they lost with that miscarriage so long ago. 'At the time I didn't feel it much. I was just worried about Chris. But now it hits home as the years go by. He or she would have been seventeen now. I wonder what it would be like to have him with us now.

'At the time of the miscarriage, oddly enough, I was working in a hospital and part of my job as theatre attendant was to supervise the disposal of foetuses after abortions – deliberate abortions. I didn't like having to take them to the incinerator at the time, though I didn't actually put them in myself. I couldn't do that job now.'

A big man, well over six feet tall, he feels considerable guilt about the miscarriage. 'A man asks himself, "Was I careful enough?"

'I've seen abortions done by the suction method in hospitals and thought it was similar to what a man does in intercourse. I used to wonder whether I might have been too much for Chris and brought on the miscarriage.'

They are both active members of the Pentecostal Church. 'Chris was there first, but I am a Christian now. I know I couldn't do that kind of work at a hospital again. General theatre, yes, but not gynaecology. I didn't agree with putting all those babies in the incinerator at the time. I certainly couldn't do it now.'

CHAPTER 9

A family affair

'Afterwards I completely neglected my husband, I didn't want him to touch me . . . He was rushed into hospital himself, suffering from colitis and had not wanted to tell me. Doctors said it was caused by all the stress at home.'

When a woman wants a child and repeatedly miscarries, her need can become so desperate that other relationships become secondary. Even her husband takes a back seat. A ruthlessness sets in as the powerful urge to conceive takes over. A woman will juggle dates and manoeuvre single-mindedly to get her partner's attentions at the right time of the month. Not for the sex act itself but for the child she so desperately needs. A fundamental urge that even the woman herself finds frightening. JACKIE had already had two sons when she found herself scheming and plotting to conceive again.

'The crazy thing is that I know that practically I would loathe having to cope with nappies and feeding again. It's just a mad emotional longing that takes over my mind.' Jackie was determined not to give in to her own 'broodiness'! She opted for sterilization

and was acutely depressed for many weeks afterwards. Her husband waited patiently for her to recover. 'He knows it will pass – that sensibly I don't really want any more children.'

Some husbands feel that they are treated as studs and that their wives are only interested in sex as a means to their maternal ends. Says Heather Robertson: 'Some men come to the miscarriage group and it emerges that there is ill feeling and resentment on the part of the husbands.' The need in a woman to go on and on trying to conceive clearly increases with recurrent miscarriages.

JOANNA, who has had fourteen miscarriages, says: 'The crazy thing is that in the beginning I didn't really want children. I was much more interested in my own life and career. But after I miscarried, I wanted a baby more and so it continued until my whole life revolved around the longing for a child.'

ANDY feels that his wife's pregnancy and miscarriage robbed them of a long period in their marriage when they might have been happy. 'We couldn't go on like that. She was so ill and I was so frightened when she was rushed to hospital. I never want us to go through all that again.'

Some women, however, know that they want children from the word 'go'. As Alison's mother says: 'She has always loved babies. When she left school, she went straight into a job as a nanny and I knew she would want a big family. If ever a girl was cut out for motherhood, it is Alison'.

When things went wrong, it was a shock for the whole family . . .

ALISON remembers: 'When I was miscarrying, my husband flaked out on the sofa. The doctor left me to look after him. The stress was all too much for him. My mother sat and cried . . .'

A miscarriage is not the concern only of the woman herself. It affects the whole family. Alison's husband Cliff backed her wholeheartedly. They both wanted children, though he might have preferred to wait a few years until they were better off materially. Alison has now had three miscarriages.

'The worry of it all robbed us of several good years. It aged me at least ten years. I find myself taking life much more seriously now.'

She was only twenty when she married. Both young, they had a perfect white wedding, a new house . . . In the beginning they had it all.

Alison is fair, warm and womanly, with softly rounded curves. She wants a baby desperately. 'That's what women are for. I just feel – let me be a woman, too.'

Alison and Cliff live in rural Lincolnshire. Miles of cabbage fields stretch from the front door; a farming area, where fertility is taken for granted. They both come from big families. She had never had any doubts about her ability to bear children. She adores them and in her work as a nanny, she brought up a small boy from the age of six months to two and a half.

This was followed by a job in a fashion shop. 'It was very trendy and I enjoyed it but I didn't really want a career.' Her husband had a good job with a national greengrocery wholesaler. She mentioned to him her hopes for a child. 'I was really in a state about it. I couldn't make him see how much I wanted a baby. But he said we could do with a bit more money, maybe a new car. In fact, we'd already bought all the essentials, even a microwave.'

They had been married just over a year when Alison started to get depressed and became quite ill. In the end, Cliff carted her off to the doctor. 'He checked me over physically, then said, "Have you got children?" At my denial, he shook his head. "Well, that's it, then; isn't it," he said.

'Cliff explained that he wanted to be in a better position before starting a family. The doctor just told him: "Well, if you're going to wait for things like that, you'll wait forever." I felt that Cliff didn't seem to care *when* we had a baby. He wanted one sometime, but didn't know exactly when, whereas I had made him the centre of my whole life. If he went out in the evening I was desperately lonely. I'd always had a child about the place – at home with my family and when I was a nanny. I just kept thinking: if anything happened to Cliff, I'll be totally alone. If I had a child, I'd have something to go on for – some point to life. I used to hate him to go out.'

After the doctor's appointment, she came off the pill and conceived immediately. But Cliff had changed his job so they decided to move 22 miles away to be nearer his work. They quickly found a house they liked and sold their own within two days. Everything was going well until, suddenly, they hit problems. 'The people we were buying from were pushing for an earlier completion date than the people buying from us could arrange their mortgage. During the first weeks of pregnancy I felt so tired, so sick in the morning. I was taking phone calls about the house before leaving for work – I could feel myself getting all tensed up and upset. One morning I sobbed to a friend on the way to work that if I didn't calm down I knew I was going to lose the baby.

'Three days before we moved house and ten weeks' pregnant, I began to get pains which gradually got stronger and closer together. I eventually lost the baby completely before the doctor arrived.

'He assured me I'd had a complete miscarriage and there was no need to go to hospital. Six days later I was still in terrific pain. As I'd never had a miscarriage before, I thought that was natural. But a friend assured me something was wrong and told me to ring the doctor. Well, I'm not the sort of person who wants to bother the doctor, so I sat for ages thinking, Shall I? Shan't I? Then I rang and said, "I'm sorry to bother you, but . . ." The doctor said there was still some of the baby left inside me and got me into hospital for a D and C.

'It was the first time I'd ever been in hospital. I came out after 48 hours.

Then we got on with packing and moving house. Nobody had warned me to take it easy so I was lifting heavy boxes, doing all sorts of things.

'Suddenly I started to haemorrhage. That was awful. I rang a girl from work and left the door open for her. She came upstairs and I shouted from the bathroom: "Don't come in here unless you can stand the sight of blood." It was just like a tap. Blood completely running. I couldn't move off the toilet. Cliff flaked out on the settee. What with travelling to work, rushing about to see me in hospital, moving house, then all this blood, he just couldn't stand it. They took me into hospital, keeping my feet up, said they'd done the first D and C wrongly. There was still some of the baby left.

'When I came out of hospital for the second time, we finally moved house. Mum and Dad came over and were marvellous. They carried the settee into the middle of the room, plonked me there and that was it. They wouldn't let me do anything. I'm very houseproud. I like to go into a house and clean it from top to bottom, then I feel it's a bit more mine. But my parents wouldn't let me.'

Alison and Cliff tried again for a baby. 'For a year it was calendars, making love when I was due to ovulate, my period was mostly late, which made it worse. I used to count years and my birthday. If I don't fall pregnant by March, 1985 ... 1986 ... 1987 ... It's everything and you feel worst of all on Christmas morning when you still haven't got a baby. All the doctors would say was, "Go away. Have a holiday. It'll happen."

'The first miscarriage wasn't so bad. I had expected to lose that one, with all the drama of house moving. People said, "Oh well, your first! There's plenty of time!" But to lose the second baby was a real blow.

'It was Saturday and I was at work. Suddenly I couldn't feel the tops of my legs. I couldn't walk. I felt paralysed and went hysterical. Cliff fetched me home and by the end of that week it was all over. I had lost the baby.

'I begged to be referred to a specialist but was told that nothing could be done until I had had at least three miscarriages. "You've just had a little more bad luck." This time I was so bitter and angry. But at the same time the guilt I'd felt about the first one was eased. The first time I'd thought it was my own fault because I had let myself get upset about moving. The second time I realized it was my own body's fault. Some consolation! Third time lucky – well, it wasn't. This time I was pregnant and happy and I thought everything would be all right. I went in quite cheerfully for a routine scan at eleven weeks. I sat chatting to another girl outside. She wasn't married.

'I knew at once when the scan technician starting tutting and sighing as he looked at the screen that something was wrong. He told me I must have my dates wrong. But there was no way I could be wrong.

'I was so aware of my body and knew exactly when the pregnancy had started. I thought "Oh God." They said they would scan me again in two weeks. I went out, in pieces, to find my poor old mum. The other girl came out of the scan next, all excited because they had found out she was expecting twins.

'I spent ages in the cubicle getting dressed, until a nurse came to find me. I asked, "Has that girl gone?" "No, she's just making her next appointment."

' "Right, I'll wait," I said . . . I couldn't go out and face her. She was carrying twins and she wasn't even married while I'd lost another one. My mum was getting upset too. She's really good. She just sits and cries with me – she feels it just as I do. We're a very close family.

'I came away in an absolute state thinking, I can't stand this for two weeks. Everybody was asking how I'd got on at the hospital. In the end I rang my own doctor and told her I thought I would go crazy. She told me to take a urine sample to the path. lab. at the hospital in the morning and ask them to do a pregnancy test. Why doesn't the hospital do a simple thing like that instead of sending you home to worry for two weeks? It's no wonder women get upset. You feel bad after the first miscarriage, worse after the second . . . and desperate after the third.

'The following day I started to bleed. My GP came round – she was marvellous. She rang the hospital to get the result straightaway. She turned to me: "I'm sorry . . ." It was negative.

'Oh God, I thought, here we go again. Mum cried again and said things like, "Never mind." When I went in to hospital again they wouldn't take it away until my womb started to contract. Apparently, it's illegal to start doing it until then. It was a dead baby, I just wanted to get it out straightaway. I was beginning to think that there was something dreadfully wrong with me and I was never going to carry. Hospitals aren't nice. At night I could hear babies crying at the other end of the ward. Some people were in for abortions. They deliberately wanted to get rid of their babies. I've been in hospital with quite a few who weren't married or who couldn't care less.'

For Alison, the worst thing was thinking she might never succeed in having a baby. 'I couldn't see a life without a baby. I couldn't come to terms with that at all. I did try to do other things. I did enjoy shop life and I loved being a nanny. In the shop a woman colleague was also trying for a baby. She had no tact whatsoever and when I came out of hospital she said, "You look really well," – I'd just come out, my hair was all greasy and I thought, "Oh God."

'In the third pregnancy when they kept waiting to be sure, and scanning again and saying the cervix wasn't open, I got really desperate. I said to the woman doctor, "You have just got to take it away." I think you should have the right to say that. But she said, "There is nothing worse than to get you down to theatre, open you up and find a perfectly normal baby there. We have to be sure."

'After I came out no one would talk about it. They might have managed a word after the first one but not after three. People just didn't know what to say.' Alison gave up her job, saying she couldn't face her former colleagues again.

The miscarriages have upset the entire family. Her mother says, 'Alison was always wanting babies, always cut out to be a mother. We never dreamed that there would be any trouble.' At the back of her mother's mind is the thought that the babies might have been handicapped in some way. Two twin sisters are 'just a little bit slow, a little bit backward'. Alison's brother and sister-in-law found themselves reluctant to tell her that they were expecting their second child.

'In the end my sister-in-law came over to tell me and she was worse than me – she absolutely sobbed . . . "We didn't know how to tell you. We didn't think it would happen so soon."

'I didn't mind people having babies, in fact. I just hated seeing women who were pregnant . . . We went on holiday one summer just after I'd lost one, and all the women seemed to be around in pretty dresses, pregnant. That was hard. Then we heard of friends who hadn't wanted a child suddenly celebrating because they were expecting. I didn't feel so good about them either, especially as he had previously told us that he didn't want any children. Suddenly, without warning, they rang and said, "Come round for a drink. We're having a baby." '

For Cliff, it has been quite a nightmare. Alison felt he was not as upset as she was about losing the pregnancies. 'Until I wrote about the experience in the newsletter of the Miscarriage Association. He sat and read it and didn't even notice the author's name until near the end. Then he started to cry and we were both able to talk about it at last.'

Worry about his wife and the miscarriages finally took their toll on Cliff. He had to go into hospital suffering from colitis, brought on, said the doctors, by stress. 'I always thought Cliff was only worried about me, not the babies, whereas I worried over each baby. I couldn't have cared less about myself.

But it seems he had been under as much pressure as I was. In fact, I promised his mother that I would only try again once more. I would never put him through it again. He doesn't tell me when he feels ill because he doesn't want to worry me. Then I worry more not knowing what is wrong with him. Our marriage is sound though, we have been through so much now.'

They were sent for genetic counselling which proved inconclusive, but now Alison is pregnant again. She is not afraid of the pain of childbirth. 'After what I've been through I think I could cope with anything. I don't mind how much pain I suffer as long as there is a baby at the end of it.'

'I had good news that I was having a baby and bad news that my dear mum was dying – all on the same day. My emotions went haywire.' For NIKKI, having a baby was a total family experience. She had always been close to her parents. Devout Catholics, they were all delighted when Nikki and her husband Kevin announced her pregnancy.

'For us it wasn't a question of saying to each other *if* we wanted children. It was a question of *when* we wanted them,' says Nikki. 'I'm baby mad! Always have been.'

In early marriage, they 'made do' with hand-me-down furniture so that they could save for a family. 'When the news broke it was Christmas. We were staying with my parents for the holiday. When I told them the baby was due it made a wonderful holiday.'

But, at twelve weeks, Nikki lost the baby. A scan at the hospital revealed that it had not survived beyond eight weeks. 'I felt sorry for the poor doctor who had to break the news.

'It must be an awful job but she was very sympathetic, knowing it was a planned pregnancy, and called it a baby, not a foetus.'

Nikki soon conceived again. A cause for celebration. 'But then we learned that my mother had cancer for the second time. She had had uterine cancer the year before, but now it was confirmed that she had lung cancer. It was so strange to get all the news on the same day. My emotions went haywire.'

Nikki's parents were a hundred miles away. Her mother had had four children and maintained an excellent relationship with them all. She stayed at home with them while they were small, then took a psychology degree and ran a home for mentally and physically handicapped children. 'She was a really strong person who took such an interest in everyone as individuals,' says Kevin. 'I always felt she valued me for myself not just because I was her son-in-law.'

The second pregnancy had its problems, including bleeding at thirteen weeks. 'I thought, Oh No. Not again!' says Nikki. 'We were giving a party that night and decided to go ahead as bed rest hadn't helped the time before. It seemed to clear up and four days later my GP examined me and reported "a womb full of baby". After that the pregnancy was fine.'

But her mother was not. Her father, himself a psychologist, confided to Nikki that he had promised her mother that, if she were going to die, he would not tell her. 'My father respected that and didn't tell her, though it was the hardest thing of all as they were very close and had no secrets. I have a feeling that she knew in her heart, anyway.

'She was super, with so many unusual interests. She had studied the history of a race course, of all things, and a museum was keen to acquire her work. People used to ask her why she did so many different things and she would say, "Because I love it." '

By September, her mother's chemotherapy treatment had ended. 'She looked well and my pregnancy was doing fine – I was feeling well and even cycling! So we all went on holiday as a family, which was brilliant,' says Nikki.

However, by Christmas her mother's health was beginning to deteriorate. The baby was due on January 22nd. 'But on January 13th I heard the terrible news that my mum had only a few days to live. Her last words to me on the phone were, "No news yet? Oh dear, no news." She sounded so weak.

'I longed for the baby to be born, but on January 23rd when he still hadn't arrived, my mother died. My dad was with her.

'On January 29th, I gave birth to a boy who was eight pounds plus (3.6 kg). Joseph Peter. My parents' first grandson. I was allowed to leave him at the hospital while I went to the funeral. A wonderful service. My mother had helped my father plan it before she died. I felt like a zombie. I heard the words: "This is the day the Lord has made. Let us rejoice and be glad in it."

'I kept thinking that I didn't believe it. I couldn't think that this was my mother's funeral. But the service was so positive. I knew that my mother was "reborn" into eternal life and I was happy for her. I really did rejoice.'

CHAPTER 10

When it happens to a teenager

'The best thing that could have happened' – Caroline's mum.

'I was sixteen, unemployed, rebellious . . . when I lost my baby, I sensed the relief all round. My mother didn't actually say, "Thank God you've lost it," but the feeling was there. Even my boyfriend seemed relieved.'

CAROLINE was sixteen and in love. 'I wanted a baby so much, to love and to hug. I was utterly miserable after the miscarriage. I had a little dog and I smothered it with attention. I felt so isolated.'

She had left school and been unable to find work. 'I see now that I was putting my parents through hell. I was involved with a man ten years older and went to live with him. My parents obviously didn't approve but dare not say so in case it drove me away completely. He couldn't marry me. He was married already.'

It never occurred to Caroline that abortion might be a possibility. 'I never had the slightest feeling of "I don't want a baby". It was wonderful, the knowledge that here inside me was a being I had created. Abortion never entered my head.'

Caroline is now 28 and can see now the affect her relationship had on her parents. 'They must have been totally devastated. But I was a rebel. I had no qualifications for a job and shouldn't have left school. But I insisted. I had dreadful hair-dos, horrendous make-up. I wore half-mast trousers and black dresses to make me look older. I hated my mother's voice. She came from the Home Counties and had had elocution lessons. She tended to sound a bit like the Queen. I hated her voice and her vowels. Why couldn't she say bath instead of barth?

'When I went to live with Jim, she said, "You are welcome in this house, but he isn't." He was a mechanic whereas my father worked in an office as a wages supervisor.

'There was a big class difference.' The baby was lost at three months. 'It wasn't painful. We were going out for the evening and we got in the bath together. I started to bleed. I said to Jim, "Go for my mum," but he wouldn't. I had to get up, dress and go to the phone box. When my mum came, she took one look and ordered me to bed. In the early hours, I woke with bad stomach pains.

The doctor came. "It's not lost yet," he said. "But the cervix is opening." I had a pregnancy test which was positive and was kept in hospital for three days. When I started to bleed heavily the nurse pulled the curtains around my bed as I was in a big public ward.

'Nobody said a word. No one said, "You've lost the baby." The nurse dressed me in a white gown and explained that I was going down to theatre. When my mother came I begged her to go to find out what was happening and she went off to look for the doctor. But when she returned she didn't say anything either.

'I was sixteen and I was frightened. Nobody was saying a word. No one said, "That's it. You've lost the baby." It was such a terrible feeling that for months afterwards I woke up screaming: "I've lost my baby." That was in 1976. I hope to God things are better now. I was in hospital for the first time in my life. Later on, my boyfriend and I split up. By this time I was having another baby. She is ten now. I went home to Mum. For a long time I was responsible for my daughter on my own.

'My mother was amazed to learn how much I had wanted that baby. People always think that at sixteen and single you'll want to get rid of it. In my case it just wasn't true.'

Caroline is now married to a policeman and her daughter has been adopted by him. She is project worker in a hostel for young offenders.

Caroline's mother is now 65. She says: 'I see now that I really didn't understand what she went through with the miscarriage. I thought at the time that it was the best thing that could have happened. After all, she couldn't marry the chap. He was already married.

'Caroline was the baby of the family, born late in life when I was 38. She was a generation away. My other children were ten and twelve when she was born. I just didn't know how to handle her. I see now that we spoiled her. She was determined she would get her way and have a baby. At that age, she was becoming a tearaway, just flitting around with no job.

'My husband never talks much, but he will always help quietly when you're in trouble. The day she left he broke down and cried. I had never seen him cry before. After she lost the baby we didn't say anything. It's always been referred to in this family as her operation, never as a baby.'

Says Caroline: 'I was grief sticken at the time. I really thought I was cracking up. I want the Miscarriage Association to cater for teenage mums as well. It mustn't just help middle-class married couples.

'Young kids as I was need help, too – possibly more.'

'I had Adam when I was eighteen and lived alone in a bedsitter. I nearly went mad in one room. No one prepares you for what life will be like after the birth. I felt so tired and weak. I was alone in Bristol. My mother lives miles away in Devon and couldn't come to see me as my brothers and sisters are too young to be left.

'When Adam was two weeks old I would cheerfully have let someone take him away. If someone had offered I would have agreed. I was just so tired.'

GEMMA has always looked after babies. When she left school she went straight to work as a mother's help.

Living in one room, it was not easy for Gemma to bring up her baby. However, she managed, and after eleven months, she was pregnant again. 'My boyfriend didn't want another, but I did. I can't explain it. I know that it's not a good idea, practically speaking, but every so often I just want another baby and that is that.'

Gemma lost the second baby at ten weeks. 'It was a shock. It had never occurred to me in a million years that anything could go wrong.'

Her third pregnancy, at nineteen, was by far the hardest experience. This time she lost the baby at 23 weeks. 'I was rushed into hospital. The baby wasn't dead then. I had felt it wriggling. But I was in labour all night. An awful labour. I just wanted it over with and it never occurred to me until I saw her that she was going to be born dead.'

The hospital, as many do these days, allowed her 23-week foetus the 'grey area' relaxation of the rule on still-births (which are supposed to start at 28 weeks) and she was able to have a photograph of the baby. She is red and thin, lying in a thoughtfully provided hospital crib, with wickerwork and lace. Gemma put a rose beside it for the photograph. Then she had a plaque made for the grave. It reads: 'Michelle Katie. Lost at Birth.'

Gemma has treasured the photographs, had Polaroid prints made at the pharmacy as often as any other proud mother. She says, 'Michelle weighed fourteen ounces (397g). She was eleven inches (28 cm) long. Her foot length was four centimetres (1½ inches). Her head circumference was eighteen centimetres (7 inches). She was small but perfect.

'The first thing I noticed when I held her were the creases at the bottom of her feet.

'I knew she would have fingernails, but for some reason, I couldn't believe the details of her wrists, ankles, knees, etc. I'd expected her to be like the pictures you see of babies in pregnancy books. Exactly baby shaped, but no details.'

With motherly pride, Gemma explains: 'She wasn't as dark as she looks in the photo. She wasn't that beetroot colour red!'

The photographs and the grave have meant a great deal to Gemma. 'I can see on the photos that she is like my son Adam in the face. I go down to the grave whenever I can and take flowers.'

'I had so many plans. No one knows how you grieve for a baby. I will always remember her fair hair and blue eyes and I'll never get over it. I may have another child, but I will never replace her!'

For Gemma the worst part was coming home to silence. 'No one mentioned what happened. No one said a word.'

CHAPTER 11

The deafening silence

'Family and friends tended to ignore what happened. My family just wouldn't talk about it. I was thrown out of hospital after a D and C and no one said a word.'

Many women complain of the constrained atmosphere they face at home after a miscarriage. As Gemma said, there was an uncanny wall of silence when she returned home after losing her baby at nineteen.

JENNY, who is 28 and a secretary, found it just as bad. She already had a daughter at school when she lost a much-wanted baby. Married for the second time, she had been pleased that her husband seemed to want children as much as she did.

'But when I came home, the loss of the child obviously hadn't been as real to him as it had to me. I felt I'd lost a baby. He had only lost the *idea* of a baby. He was quite helpful, but there seemed nobody for me to turn to.

'One of the hardest things was to tell people what had happened. I couldn't use the word "miscarriage".

'The worst thing was to go into the school playground, to see all the pregnant mums and the new babies.

'You feel so dreadful. I would just look at them and think, "I could drown them, strangle them." It's just that they've got something you haven't. It seems so unfair!

'I wrote to my sisters, telling them what had happened. They didn't call and I just felt they could have rung to ask, "Are you OK?" When people did talk to me they just said, "You are young. You can try again." I was 28 and thought that was quite old to be having a baby. People also said, "Be thankful for the one you've got," which didn't seem to help much either.'

KIM, 28, happy in her first pregnancy, was sick with disappointment when she lost the baby at twelve weeks.

'I saw the foetus and kept it in a dish for the doctor to see. He glanced at it to see that I had had a complete miscarriage then he casually flushed it down the loo.

'I suppose it was the only thing to do with it but I would have liked the chance to decide for myself, even if I had only buried it in the garden!'

When it happened, Kim was furious

about the lack of understanding all round. 'Life is absolute hell. I feel hurt, angry and completely in the dark. If anyone else says, "Never mind. You can have another," or "It was nature's way of telling you something was wrong with the baby," I shall SCREAM!!'

She was lucky enough to become pregnant again quickly afterwards and to have a son. But this has in no way lessened her anger. 'People who were good friends still cross the road to avoid speaking to me.

'It made it worse that it happened just before Christmas and I came out to celebrations of a baby's birth. Only my mother understood and told me to talk to her and cry whenever I wanted. Everyone else expected me to get over it in a week.

'When I got pregnant again they were all busy saying that I was bound to be all right as I was expecting another but that does not change anything. The birth of another baby is wonderful, but it does not change the grief you feel for the child you've lost.'

After a miscarriage, it is very important for a woman to be able to talk about what has happened.

Dr R. T. Corney and Dr F. T. Horton have pointed out in the *American Journal of Psychiatry* that women frequently suffer unresolved grief after miscarriage, which they describe as a 'syndrome of anger, agitation and an inclination towards self damage'.[7]

Dr J. A. Stack, in the *American Family Practitioner* described unresolved grief after miscarriage as characterized by 'vivid, crystal-clear memory and frequent flashing through the mind of the events surrounding the miscarriage'.[8] He said that women often have a persistent emotional reaction when talking about the loss and a welling up of emotion when subsequent crises occur.

After miscarriage a woman is grieving just as much as she might after a family death. She must work through the whole process of grieving.

Dr E. Lindemann, in the *American Journal of Psychiatry* pointed out as long ago as 1944[9] that it is important for a grieving patient to accept the pain of bereavement and express her sorrow and sense of loss.

Understandably, a busy obstetrician cannot devote hours to the listening and encouragement she needs, but support needs to come from someone. If nurses and the family doctor can't get involved, then clearly the support should come from the family.

If women are not given this help, morbid grief can go on for years and ruin their lives.

So what can a family do to help?

1 Listen!! Workers in the field emphasize that a woman will be constantly turning over this experience in her mind. She will probably have a lot of grief, frustration and bitterness to vent.

2 Ask how she feels – a few weeks later as well as immediately afterwards. **Give her the chance to talk.**

3 Keep in touch. Sometimes, the worst period is not at first when she feels numb, but later, when the shock wears off and the fact of her loss hits her.

JENNY had had two or three days of knowing that her baby was dead and that she had to have a D and C to remove it, so the shock wore off while she was still in hospital. 'I had a lovely nurse with me. She just put her arm around me and I really sobbed. I lay in bed for three hours afterwards and just cried.'

4 If someone in your family has lost a baby, don't feel you have to supply answers to every question. She may ask, 'Why me?' and there won't be a clear-cut medical answer. Expect her to burst into tears for all kinds of reasons – just walking past Mothercare or seeing a woman in a maternity dress. After a miscarriage some women boast, 'I can spot a pregnant woman in a crowded street at five miles off!'

5 Don't forget the partner – a man may be feeling just as rough about it, but will be trying not to show his feelings.

When his wife had a miscarriage, ALAN tried to bottle up his feelings and became possessive. He didn't like her to go out, even for a harmless game of badminton. He says: 'We tried to talk, but we couldn't. We would just argue. Then one night I admitted to her that I couldn't feel the same as she did. I told her to talk to me and after that we seemed to talk, to cry, even become a little bit closer because of what happened.'

6 Don't offer clichés like, 'You can always have another.' No one can guarantee that.

7 Whatever you do, don't pretend it never happened. Put the ball in her court, with a 'How do you feel now?' and let her talk it out *if she wants to*.

8 Above all, don't tell her to 'Pull yourself together.' The Miscarriage Association always gives 'permission to grieve' and the chance to cry.

Often, breaking the news of a miscarriage is hardest of all when you have to tell other children who were hoping for a little brother or sister. If, like me, you have been rash enough to tell them too early, obviously you are obliged to tell them when the baby is dead.

TRACEY had nieces and nephews who knew she was expecting. When she lost the pregnancy she explained straightaway that the baby was dead. 'I found it easiest to explain that he had gone to Jesus,' says Tracey. 'They seemed to accept that, as they could link it with the recent death of my father. They tended to say, "The baby's died and gone to Jesus with Uncle Jo," and that satisfied them.'

The Pregnancy and Infant Loss Center in the USA explain the situation in an illustrated children's booklet. They put the facts simply: 'The baby has died in Mom's tummy.'

The most important thing is to explain. Trying to keep them in the dark only causes confusion. They worry much more if they see their mother in tears and don't know the reason!

If you are a grandparent

Grandparents often come in for criticism for 'saying the wrong thing' when a daughter miscarries, but often they face a nightmare in trying to be helpful.

The Miscarriage Association in the UK and the Pregnancy and Infant Loss Center in the USA bear this in mind and put out special leaflets to be read by other members of the family.

NANCY in California splashed out a hundred dollars on a lace-covered dress for her still-born baby to wear for the burial. Nancy's mother thought she was mad and described it as 'a terrible waste of money'. But Nancy explained that she would never have the chance to dress up her little girl again. It was a once-only party dress and the simple purchase of it had brought Nancy much comfort.

Advice to grandparents includes: Make a ritual of the baby's death with pictures of it if possible, photos from a memorial service . . . use his or her name whenever possible . . . Try not to take over arrangements.

Your children are adults. Let them decide what is the best thing to do about a funeral.

Communicate with your children. Tell them how you are feeling and help them to understand your own loss and helplessness. **Don't try to take their pain away**. They need their pain and tears. Just be by their side.

Helpful comments

'It's hard to know what to say. I feel so helpless.' Be honest, but let them know you care.

'I never knew my grandchild and that disappoints me.' Feel free to share your personal sorrow. This cements relationships.

'I'm here to listen and I want to help.' Be available. Be supportive. Don't make judgements about how they handle the crisis and the decisions they make.

'I miss . . .' Use his name if he had one.

'I'm proud of you.' Their self-esteem will be low. Your encouragement will give them strength.

Comments which might not be helpful

'You can always have another.' – Who can promise that? In any case, it would not replace the child they have just lost.

'Be thankful for the other children you've got.' – When you've just lost one, it's hard to be grateful for the others. That may come later, but *not now*.

'It will be easier to get over this, as it was only a miscarriage (or) the baby did not live very long.' – That is not fair. When you love someone, even if only in hopes and dreams, their loss is very painful. The length of time is irrelevant.

If they have a second pregnancy, don't have endless inquests about 'what went wrong' last time. Be hopeful. Wish them luck. Share their happiness with congratulations, presents and faith in the future.

CHAPTER 12

The harder they try . . .

'We always planned on having children. A couple of kids would have been smashing. I was twenty when I got married and we've now been trying to have a baby for ten years. We've got an infertility problem, yet I've had miscarriages. It doesn't make sense, does it? . . .'

BABS is a professional tutor recently promoted in her job. 'I put in for promotion wanting to be busy, to take my mind off all this.' Babs has had three miscarriages. 'The first one was the greatest shock of my life. The initial reactions of bewilderment, despair and depression gradually developed into anger and bitterness – because there was no obvious reason!'

After three miscarriages, Babs and her accountant husband Tish underwent tests to try to find the solution to their 'unexplained infertility'.

These included a laparoscopy, blood tests, post-coital tests – where doctors check immediately after intercourse to find out exactly what is happening. Babs went through the routine of taking her temperature every morning to pinpoint ovulation days and the best time to make love. She had a course of Clomid to stimulate ovulation and was on fertility drugs for a time – the sort which are associated with multiple births. These included Human Chorionic Gonadotrophin and Perganol (Human Menopausal Gonadotrophin). None of these treatments seemed to help. All tests were normal. Eventually she was put on the waiting list for a test-tube baby – *in vitro* fertilization. 'I have been warned that if we are accepted for test-tube baby treatments it will mean moving down to London to be near Hammersmith hospital during the time of the treatment and actually being in hospital for a good part of the time with complete bed rest. Three months in bed for a start!'

At the age of 33, though, she feels it will be worth it. 'I don't want to become about 45 and look back with regret thinking I haven't tried all possibilities. Our whole life has been geared to having a family. All our friends are going in for children successfully. I am godmother to some of them. After my miscarriages, I became acutely sensitive to anything to do with babies. The sight of a pregnant woman caused bitter tears.'

She has tried to adjust her life to

childlessness. 'I got the promotion I wanted in my career, so that I am really busy all day and genuinely don't have too much time to dwell on things. Superficially, I'm learning to enjoy the freedom of not having children. More time and money. Other mums envy us, they say. We can go on holidays abroad and all that!'

Babs has become active in the Miscarriage Association and runs a group. 'The letters in the newsletter seemed to upset me sometimes. I would read a letter describing a traumatic experience of miscarriage but often the writer's letter went on to say that shortly afterwards she had a successful pregnancy. My big problem is getting pregnant in the first place.'

Sadly, it is a fact that the more difficulty a couple have in conceiving, the more likely they are to lose the pregnancy.

Says Babs: 'We try all the time, yet it seems as if with each pregnancy the time it takes to conceive becomes longer. I began to think of all kinds of medical reasons. Was it from stress, from being constantly upset because I couldn't get pregnant, then upset again because I lost the pregnancy? Every time we go to the christening of someone else's baby, the tears well up.'

Babs feels that the constant strain of temperature charts, letting your calendar dates govern when you have intercourse does not really do much for a husband. 'I think many men begin to feel that it is mechanical love-making. When you have to – not when you want to! We've been lucky and my husband has adapted more to life without children than I have, but I can under-

stand why some marriages suffer under the strain!'

Current trends towards late babies can have their problems. FRAN, who lives in an idyllic spot on the coast near Plymouth, where her husband is a boat builder, put off having children until her early thirties. 'I suppose it was because we wanted to get the house right. John wanted to do it all himself and he fitted cupboards everywhere and built a conservatory. I was working as a nursery nurse and it never occurred to me I would have any problems in having children.'

But she found it took longer to conceive than she had imagined and was eventually put on Clomid to stimulate ovulation as she didn't seem to be ovulating every month.

She was 36 by the time she conceived and lost the baby at twelve weeks. Her D and C brought complications and she finally sued the hospital successfully for negligence.

Her second pregnancy two years later was also lost at twelve weeks. 'The hospital treatment was a nightmare. They had lost my papers. I had to go into a geriatric ward as there was no other bed and was eventually moved to another hospital altogether to have my D and C the next day!'

Fran had nearly given up. 'We wanted a child so much, especially as John is an only child and it was his parents' only chance of a grandchild.

With her third pregnancy, however, the consultant seemed to be 'keeping an eye' on her and her daughter Jayne was born. 'I'm forty now and I won't push my luck to try again.

'I also think I'm a lot more tired than

a younger mother might be. I had no idea it was all going to take so long, that having a baby in my thirties was going to be such a problem.

'I don't feel guilty because Jayne will be an only child. I'm a professional child-minder now, working at home, and there will always be plenty of children here. She won't be lonely.'

No matter how fashionable it becomes to have late babies, there are still medical problems. There is no escaping the fact that it becomes much harder to conceive when you are in your thirties or forties. Even in your early-thirties it can take up to two years. Fertility falls off after the age of 30 and, after 35, the chances of giving birth to an abnormal child increase, though with tests such as amniocentesis now available, this worry is somewhat reduced.

SHERRI at 38 married for the second time. She desperately wanted children by her new husband, who is six years younger and an editor at a top London news agency.

She already had two children, aged 16 and 11, by her previous marriage. But her first pregnancy with her new partner ended in miscarriage.

Doctors discovered that it was a hydatidiform mole pregnancy. 'This was odd,' says Sherri, 'as I had not had more sickness than usual, as you would expect in a molar pregnancy. My stomach felt very big and empty and I had a lot of wind. But I certainly didn't feel particularly sick.' (See Chapter 5 for details of molar pregnancy.)

She was advised to wait a year before trying again because of the risk of cancer following a molar pregnancy. She became pregnant again at the end of that year but miscarried at eleven weeks. A third pregnancy ended in miscarriage at eight weeks. It was possibly a blighted ovum. Her fourth pregnancy ended at sixteen weeks.

'We were both upset about this as the scan had shown everything to be OK just the day before. My husband was devastated. Obviously, at 32 and with no children, it would be nice for him to have one.'

At this stage she was referred to St Mary's Hospital, Paddington (in London) for immunotherapy. But a fifth pregnancy, at 41, ended in seven weeks.

'I am getting more philosophical about it now, but a year ago I was terribly upset,' says Sherri. 'I think my chances are slim now. But we shall go on trying.'

KAREN is a student of agricultural research. Her husband is a farmer. They have been trying so hard to conquer Karen's fertility problem that at one stage she was expecting triplets! The idea of a multiple birth made John a little nervous. 'You'd think he would be hardened to this sort of thing in animals but he is not. He was quite happy when we thought I was having twins. Ideal, really, he said, but how were we going to cope with triplets?'

It all began seven years previously when Karen was concerned because her periods had stopped. She was given a 'fertility' drug, Perganol, to stimulate ovulation. She conceived three years later at the age of 28, but at thirteen weeks she miscarried a 'normal-looking' foetus. Her treatment continued after a three-month break. She conceived again, but was bleeding on and off from Day 28 onwards.

Perganol is human menopausal gonadotrophin, a natural hormone taken from the urine of post-menopausal women. It is used to treat infertility and carries the possibility of multiple births. It is the drug that caused so much 'fertility drug' furore when it was first introduced, but the possibility of quads and quintuplets is now much lessened as doctors are more experienced in its use and correct dosage.

However, Karen soon found that she was carrying three potential babies – three embryos – and John was 'a bit worried'. The idea of twins had appealed much more to both of them.

In fact, all three embryos failed to develop, and at ten weeks a D and C was performed to removed them.

At that time, Karen was seeing a top London specialist and spent eight months travelling up and down to London from her home in Lincolnshire, a 300-mile round trip, often ten times a month!

She conceived again but started to bleed on Day 28 when her period would have been due. She was given huge doses of progesterone by injection and the bleeding eventually stopped.

She saw an embryo with a beating heart on the scan at six and a half weeks, but by eight weeks this had gone. Again a missed miscarriage and a further D and C.

'Both my specialists, at home and in London, put all three miscarriages down to bad luck,' says Karen. 'They said that they were all for different reasons. They both seemed to feel that the progesterone had merely prolonged the agony.

'My specialist at home suggested HCG

(Human Chorionic Gonadotrophin), another fertility drug obtained from the urine of pregnant women. But my specialist in London said that this wouldn't work.'

In the middle of it all, Karen felt the only course open to her was 'to try and try again'. She kept reminding herself that many people did carry a baby to full term, though she says she nearly gave up many times. 'I got so nervous, hardly daring to move when I got pregnant and terrified of going to the toilet in case I saw the first drop of blood. I had abandoned my career as I was devoting all my time to travelling and seeing doctors. I began to wonder whether I was doing the right thing.'

Further treatment with Perganol brought another pregnancy and this time her specialist 'at home' gave her the injections of HCG they had discussed. She needed three injections a week until she was fourteen weeks' pregnant and her husband was shown how to do them for her.

All went well until 38 weeks, when a scan showed that the baby was not growing properly. After three days' bed rest in hospital, the scan still showed up the same problem. There were fears that the placenta was failing so she was induced. But during delivery it was noted that the baby's heart rate had dropped and an emergency Caesarean was done. Luckily she was able to have the operation with an epidural so that she could be aware of what was happening.

'So the birth of Abby was a wonderful experience. My husband was conned by the doctors into staying with me throughout the operation as they told him it would help me. In fact although he's a farmer he's not a bit tough when it comes to the sight of blood! This way he was able to be with me and see the operation happening if he wanted. But he didn't *have* to look!

'He was lucky and saw the baby first. Now he thinks she is wonderful and he wants another. But she's still only four months old . . . I say it's all right for him!'

CHAPTER 13

A survey of reactions

So many women seem to feel the need, after miscarriage, to write to the Miscarriage Association to pour out their feelings of bewilderment that I asked them to complete a small questionnaire for me.

Asked to describe their opinions of the way they were treated by the professionals, only 22 per cent said they felt their care had been adequate.

In medicine, miscarriage is normally considered a minor problem. 'It is hardly life threatening and diagnosis and therapy are straightforward . . .', says Professor H. J. Huisjes, Professor of Obstetrics and Gynaecology at the University of Groningen, the Netherlands.[10] He describes the dilemma of an obstetrician who has no insight into the causes of miscarriage, when he is faced with the 'despair of women suffering miscarriage after miscarriage'.

Doctors themselves may feel upset over miscarriage. As long ago as 1977, an editorial in the Lancet on the 'abhorrence of still-birth'[11] called the experience of 'death in utero' extraordinarily chilling and repugnant.

In our survey, 80 per cent were left feeling angry and of those 66 per cent replied that they felt their treatment had been poor; 16 per cent described it as 'very helpful'. Four per cent were 'just resigned, but content that everything had been done'. Most complained about the lack of counselling. 'It was obvious,' said one woman, 'that the staff regarded it as a minor operation to be finished as soon as possible and the patient released.'

Londoner Christine, who has had three miscarriages, was concerned about the lack of privacy. 'Afterwards the consultant talked to us all together in a group. Instead of a private consultation, he talked to several patients at one go. We could all hear what he was telling the others. He tore a strip off a young girl who was having an abortion. He discussed my miscarriage . . . it was all most embarrassing. A diabolical experience!'

Staff were criticized by many patients for giving the impression that a miscarriage in the first three months is really 'nothing much'.

Yet, there seems a growing interest on the part of hospitals to appreciate more the emotions of women after miscarriage.

Many women reported that a hospital had allowed the compassion of a 'grey area' so that a miscarriage at nineteen weeks could have the privileges which, strictly speaking, are really only for still-births of 28 weeks. A Polaroid photo-graph of the dead infant was sometimes available, plus a burial if they felt it would help. Gemma described the burial of her 23-week gestation daughter as 'something I will always remember'.

Lorraine wished she had asked for her 26-week gestation baby to be buried. She was given the choice but advised against it on the grounds that it would upset her. 'It upsets me more now because only myself and my husband remember Nia. We have no picture or gravestone – or anything – as evidence of her life and death,' says Lorraine.

Only one woman said she would not have wanted a burial. She was offered it by a member of the hospital staff after her baby miscarried at eighteen weeks. 'The thought of a funeral after all I'd been through just upset me. I just wanted to go home and forget what had happened.'

'I have never come across a reaction against a burial,' says Heather Robert-son. 'I just hope it didn't prevent that hospital from offering it to other mothers. The girls I deal with break their hearts – they want their babies to be buried so much.

'In fact, we have offered a pretty crib to one hospital so that miscarried babies can be photographed in it.' She also sees it as a breakthrough that she has been invited to talk to medical staff about the needs of women after miscar-riage, as have Miscarriage Association members in other parts of the UK.

The medical attitude to miscarriage needs to be revised, say many women. Nicola, a nurse in the north of England and in Scotland, says, 'As a student I was taught nothing about miscarriage. It was mentioned as a side issue – something that happens *sometimes* – but no one told me how to deal with it, or what the feelings of the patient might be.'

ANNE, who is a translator, has had four miscarriages. She described her doctor's attitude as 'totally useless'. She feels that it is in the peculiar area of miscarriage that many doctors fail, although they are excellent in every other area of medicine.

Says Anne: 'I just did not understand it. My doctor is brilliant on everything with me and terrific with the children's problems now they are here. But when I had a miscarriage he completely failed me and I got no support at all.

'It was almost as if he were apologiz-ing, saying, "Look, I can't do much with the resources I have available. You'll have to go home and get on with it. There is nothing I can do for you." He didn't actually say those words but that was the feeling I was left with.'

Anne had three miscarriages at home. 'It wasn't until the third one when I was in a lot of pain that my husband made a fuss and said to the doctor, "Don't you think she has suffered enough?" Then they got me in for a D and C.

'I had thought that once I had three miscarriages, that that was the magic number and they would refer me. But the doctor said, "Look, I've got one woman who has had six miscarriages. How can I refer you?"'

'So I used the private medical insurance scheme which we were in and was able to see a gynaecologist privately. He was the same one I had seen under the NHS, but he only had about ten seconds for me in the hospital. I saw him privately and he had time to talk. When I conceived again I was scanned at six weeks and saw a live foetus.

'But at eight weeks he had disappeared. Another missed miscarriage and D and C. After that, I took along a magazine cutting about St Mary's [St Mary's Hospital in Paddington, London] and he said, "All right. Give it a go," and referred me to St Mary's for immunotherapy.'

Anne was lucky. She conceived immediately after the immunization and now has two daughters, Jenny, three and Sarah, ten months.

'The immunotherapy treatment was absolutely brilliant. Without it I would still be trying now, perhaps having miscarriage after miscarriage.

'After a while, it is a compulsion to keep trying because as the months go by you know that only a baby is going to make up for what you've lost. I am broody again now although I have two daughters. On a sunny afternoon I go shopping and see all the prams on parade. All the babies being promenaded. I see branches of Mothercare on every street. I come home feeling really clucky!'

The problem of doctors' apparent difficulty in coping with miscarriage has been highlighted by members of the Miscarriage Association who are compiling a Good Doctors' Guide – a roll of honour which lists the names of all doctors who are helpful in miscarriage!

On this Roll of Honour, says LIANE, should go her family doctor. Liane reported to the survey that her treatment at the time of a miscarriage was 'very helpful'.

'My woman doctor was wonderful and the staff at the hospital couldn't have been better,' says Liane, who lost her first baby at twelve weeks.

'I started to bleed a little and told the doctor. When it got really heavy two days later I rang her first thing. She was just opening surgery for the day but in ten minutes the door bell rang and there she was. She phoned for an ambulance, helped me pack a few things, waited while it arrived then went back – late – to start her surgery. She couldn't have been kinder.

'At the hospital, which was a big London teaching hospital, they had to put me in a surgical ward as there was no room in Gynae., so when I actually lost the baby, into a bedpan, a very young student nurse was with me. She couldn't have been more than about eighteen and I felt sorry for her. The last thing you expect on a surgical ward is to cope with a miscarriage.

'But she was super. She asked me whether I wanted to see the baby. I had a look at him and I was glad I did. He was so perfect. I cried a bit and the student nurse sat with me. A young doctor was good, too. He was very kind and patted my hand. Then, a Staff Nurse came and she cried too!! They were lovely people.

'It's nearly four years ago now, but I often think about that day and how good they were – that poor girl, what a shock for her!'

Lianne was 27 when it happened. Fertility problems followed. A laparoscopy showed up a slight tubal blockage and after treatment she eventually got her wish – a daughter.

When SYLVIA took part in the survey she said she felt the treatment she had received at the time of her five miscarriages was poor. It had left her feeling sad, disappointed and bitter.

Sylvia is no stranger to the hospital world as her husband is an ambulance driver. 'But I was horrified at the attitude of the staff to miscarriage. They all seemed to think it was nothing to worry about. Just a miscarriage!'

She had had a difficult first pregnancy at 34 with her son Paul. 'There was no time for an episiotomy and I was badly torn and needed a lot of stitches afterwards. I had been induced and he arrived very fast in an hour and a half.'

Sylvia thinks this may have caused problems with further pregnancies as she lost the next baby at fifteen and a half weeks.

'I just woke up one morning, went to the bathroom and found I was losing the complete sac, bag of waters. It was half in and half out of me, with the foetus of the baby, a little boy, inside.

'I had had no warning of threatened miscarriage, but the doctor didn't believe me and thought I must have known. They all seemed to think I should have known. My own doctor had to come to me. He tried to pull out the placenta and caused a severe haemorrhage. They took the foetus

away in my husband's ambulance and I expect they incinerated it though they said that tests were usually done.'

Her second miscarriage was at eighteen and a half weeks and happened in spite of the cervical stitch which had been inserted to stop her miscarrying.

'That was another little boy. I named him Graham. The other one was Richard.

'The next three miscarriages were just early ones, so obviously I didn't know what sex they were and could only think of them by the months of the year. I always thought of one as Noel.' The attitude of the medics she describes as, 'totally unhelpful. Last time I was pregnant, my consultant had written to my own doctor and he said to me, "Come back again in four weeks if you are still pregnant." As if he knew I wouldn't be. They gave me nothing. No help or interest.'

Sylvia is now 44 and has given up hope of another baby.

SANDRA, who is 28, was also disappointed about the care she received in her two miscarriages – one at ten and one at twelve weeks.

'My own doctor is ideal and the nurses were fine and helpful. It was the hospital doctors who were so abrupt and uninterested. I understand. I know they are busy. But it would have been nice to see someone who could really discuss the case. I felt it was just another miscarriage to them. Not important.'

Some give up

After several miscarriages, some women pull out. Swedish-born Ingrid has had three miscarriages. 'No one took any notice. It was a kind of medical shrug of the shoulders after all of them. On the third one I had kept the products of conception in case someone could test them to see what had gone wrong. I was upset when a nurse just threw them away.'

INGRID is a nurse herself, working in a British hospital. 'I know when medical staff are just not interested. All three miscarriages left me with a big question mark. As I have had tubal surgery, I would like to have known whether the problems were related.

'I was working in a big orthopaedic unit at the time and I did wonder whether the physical work had anything to do with it – all the lifting and so on.'

Ingrid and her husband, who is in banking, have decided not to try any further for a family of their own, but are being assessed for adoption.

VALERIE, who is a college lecturer, has had three miscarriages. 'The first time I felt that I was losing the baby but he could be clearly distinguished on the scan, jumping around. The staff, seeing me among the conveyor belt of happy pregnancies, just said, "It'll be all right." But it wasn't.'

She felt her treatment at the time of her miscarriages was poor. 'I honestly felt that no one was terribly interested. After the third miscarriage, I had immunotherapy treatment. But I was unlucky and lost another baby.'

Valerie and her husband, who is a solicitor, have now given up. 'It had interrupted my career and, anyway, my husband was never as keen as I was. I'm busy with my career. I've taken up aerobics and we have a boat on the canal, so lots of friends with children love to bring them on the boat with us. I spent eight years trying for a baby. At 38, I've given up.'

'My doctor held my hand . . .'

TINA has lost four babies. Three times, no foetal heart was shown up on the scan. 'My doctors were absolutely marvellous. When my consultant had to tell me that for the fourth time I was going to miscarry, he held my hand and broke the news to me gently in a small room. They were absolutely marvellous.

'My husband sobbed every time the doctors had to tell him, "There is no baby." '

Tina always seemed to be pregnant at the same time as colleagues in the bank where she works, or at the time that close relatives were also pregnant. 'Then they would go ahead to have successful births, bring their babies to show off and I'd have to take it.'

At 25, Tina had just had another miscarriage when her sister-in-law was rushed in for an emergency Caesarean. 'They rang to say she had had the baby and was fine,' says Tina. 'I was delighted for them and rushed out to tell Peter my husband, who was outside cleaning the car. I fell into his arms and cried my eyes out.

'After that we decided not to try any

more for babies. We bought a new car, I got new clothes. We decided not to worry any more about making love at the right time. If it happens, it happens, we said.

'But I wasn't going to be obsessed about it any more . . . after all, you don't always feel like it just when the calendar says you should.'

Obsessed or not, Tina is now a proud mother – of Becky and Emily!

CHAPTER 14

Treatments: the breakthrough

'It was such a fight to get this new "miracle" treatment. I fought one long battle to get attention – but I knew immunotherapy was my only chance of a child.'

SARAH has a baby now. Lucy is six weeks old and adored by both her parents. A triumph, not merely for the medical world but for her mother's determination. Like most of us, Sarah read in a newspaper about the new immunological work which was bringing hope to thousands of women who had suffered recurrent miscarriages.

But how do you get this kind of top specialist help when you live in the suburbs and your doctor won't even refer you to a gynaecologist? At 28, Sarah felt she had to assert herself. 'I hated to have to make a fuss, but I felt I was getting older all the time. I had had only two miscarriages and my doctor wasn't keen to refer me. The magic number is three and until you have had three they just send you home with encouraging noises – to keep trying!

'Luckily – or unluckily! – after twisting my doctor's arm to get an appointment with a local gynaecologist I had to wait six months to see him. I had

a third miscarriage during that time. He said, "Oh good. We can investigate if you've had three." ' She took a cutting from a newspaper about immunotherapy and explained what she wanted. It was agreed that she should be referred to St Mary's Hospital, Paddington, in London, after blood tests were taken locally. But there were hold-ups. The results of her husband's blood tests were lost – vital tests for AIDS and hepatitis. It was all taking months and Sarah worried. She phoned the hospital during her lunch break at the school where she teaches. 'It was horrendous. I couldn't get through for ages, and when I finally got the right department, a junior doctor told me that my gynaecologist was away for six weeks. I must wait, he said.

'I just knew I had to do battle. How could they be so casual and waste time? I was 28 and growing older every day. "I haven't got time to wait six weeks," I said. "I want something done *now*."

'The doctor – he was a senior registrar – said it was more than his job was worth to go over the gynaecologist's head. "Anyway," he said, "We're very busy here."

'I exploded. "I'm busy, too. I'm a teacher ringing you in my lunch hour. Surely that's what your job is all about. To do something for people like me." So he came round, started to call me Sarah and things began to move!'

After blood tests had been taken locally, Sarah and her husband were invited to spend the day at St Mary's for further treatment. When they had both got the day off work and arrived there they found that their records hadn't. So Sarah got them photocopied herself. When she was finally found to be suitable for the immunotherapy treatment, her husband Paul gave a pint of blood. White blood cells were removed from it, filling half a test-tube, and Sarah was injected with them. She had five injections in her arm. Soon after, she found she was pregnant.

'Just a day in London for both of us. The immunization took so little time.

'Then I came back home to have my antenatal appointments at my local hospital. As I was on this treatment I was quite a celebrity!'

For the first few weeks she had a weekly scan to reassure her that the foetus was progressing normally. She also saw the consultant every time. When the baby was due, she was induced. 'The consultant said, "I'm going to get a bit twitchy if we don't," and Sarah weighed in at 7lb 4oz (3.28kg) – a good weight for a smallish mother.

'Even my husband was thrilled. He had been pretty laid back about it at the beginning. It was more difficult for him to get time off – he's a teacher too – and I don't think men ever feel quite so involved as women. I just wish I hadn't had to make so much fuss to get my own way. But Lucy was worth it.'

Immunotherapy: the magic answer?

The treatment which gave Sarah her baby and has also brought success to thousands of others who had given up hope of a child is **immunotherapy**. A pioneer in the UK is Richard Beard, Professor of Obstetrics and Gynaecology at St Mary's Hospital, Paddington in London.

Professor Beard has worked closely on immunology research with Professor James Mowbray, Professor of Experimental Pathology. Says Professor Beard: 'We had found a problem in medicine that we needed to sort out. We worked away to try to help those women who

miscarry frequently.'

Himself the father of boys ('after three very robust pregnancies') he had become alarmed by the suffering of those women who had often lost up to twelve or fifteen pregnancies. His team had been studying their emotional response. 'Some of them become severely disturbed. They often complain of a dull ache in the pit of the stomach. "Once I feel that," they would tell me, "I know I am going to miscarry again." Their emotions had sparked off a physical response. The uterus was contracting just as muscles elsewhere in the body contract – as a shoulder might contract, for instance. Then they would soon begin to bleed and lose yet another pregnancy. Anxiety and tension was triggering it, so we must try to help them learn to relax.'

Professor Beard and his team also wanted to solve a mystery. 'We had found a question we couldn't answer. We needed to sort out why some women were repeatedly miscarrying.'

The main mystery that Professor Beard set out to solve was why some women apparently reject their own babies and put an end to the pregnancy with a miscarriage. In pregnancy, 50 per cent of the fertilized egg is not from the mother but from the father. By a special reaction, she does not reject it as 'foreign' as her body might reject a transplanted heart or liver. But some women apparently don't have the special protective mechanism to keep the foetus and they reject it.

The breakthrough was the discovery that if a woman was injected with some of her partner's white blood cells she did not reject the pregnancy. In other words, she could actually be immunized against miscarriage.

The procedure is simple. The couple – as in Sarah and Paul's case – answer a full questionnaire about their history then, if they are suitable, blood tests are carried out in their home area, to make sure they are not suffering from conditions such as hepatitis or AIDS. Once this is done, they must both spend a day at St Mary's, so that blood can be taken from the man and the wife can be immunized.

This is normally done while she is not pregnant and can conceive during the next few weeks and perhaps have a booster immunization later.

Results have been impressive. First reported in the *Lancet* as having a 77 per cent success rate,[12] they have now been quoted as high as 85 per cent by some doctors.

The take-home-baby rate

Professor Beard says, 'We now can give you a take-home baby rate of between 70 and 75 per cent. We have found a treatment which seems to work but we don't know why. The theory is that we're all made up of a mass of antigens, part of the HLA system which sits on chromosome 6. It is suggested that some couples share important antigens so the same immune protection which normal pregnancies get is not accorded to these people.

'The opposite of this is when you get Hybrid Vigour. This is when you get two people who are very antigenically dissimilar. They have a baby which grows larger and stronger than normal. This is well recognized and is why people talk about "introducing new blood into the stock".

'The problem is that we don't yet know the specific antigen–antibody reaction which we think is protecting the developing conceptus (the baby). All tissues have antigens against which antibodies can be formed. But there are one or two areas in the body where they don't seem to have detectable antigens on the surface. One of these is the placenta and its trophoblast – the bit of the placenta which invades the mother – which we can't isolate. The work here which Professor Mowbray is doing suggests that we may be near to finding these specific antigen–antibody complexes.

'So what we're doing when we treat women with their partner's white cells is giving them an extra-strong boost to try to stimulate the immune response which we think is protecting the pregnancy.' Professor Beard likes to immunize a woman before she becomes pregnant; otherwise it has to be done within ten days of the first period being missed.

TERRY, who had had nine miscarriages at a very early stage, found she was pregnant soon after St Mary's agreed to take her for this treatment. 'I panicked, phoned up to say, "I'm pregnant and I'm going to lose it." '

She was immunized in time – approximately fourteen days after conception. 'Within about three hours my body felt completely different. I felt I was really pregnant, with aching breasts. And I felt sick. It was wonderful.' Thirty-seven weeks later she gave birth to a healthy boy, weighing 8lbs 8ozs (3.85kg).

Is there any risk of developing abnormal babies with immunotherapy? Babies who would otherwise miscarry? A disturbing report from the US suggested that injecting white blood cells into the skin might be compromising the baby's development in later pregnancy. They reported very low-weight babies born at full term. But at St Mary's this problem has not arisen. A much larger dose of the cells is given, predominantly intravenously, and birth weights are comparable with those of untreated women.

Women are screened very thoroughly before being accepted for treatment, so that any chromosomal or genetic ab-normalities show up. This is to alleviate any fears that defective embryos, which would normally miscarry, might go on to develop. Again, the rate of defective babies, abnormalities and still-births is no higher than normal.

Some immunologists in the UK are trying an alternative method of immunotherapy. Professor Peter Johnson of Liverpool University has achieved a success rate similar to St Mary's by using another technique. Instead of using white blood cells, he takes the outer membrane of key placental cells – the critical point of contact between mother and foetus – and gives them to women in transfusion form. This is a more complicated method than using white blood cells, but Professor Johnson thinks it may be safer. 'White blood cells are living cells and we do not want to sensitize women against other factors.'

For some couples, success with immunotherapy is quite a long and arduous achievement. LIZ and MIKE had heard about it on television. At 37, Liz's recurrent miscarriages had led them to give up hope, but specialists at a hospital in Southampton were enthusiastic about the treatment and Liz was immunized.

At 23 weeks pregnant, everything was going fine until she suffered a heart attack. This was purely bad luck, nothing at all to do with the immunotherapy treatment, but it meant she had to stay in hospital.

She spent the next few weeks in a cardiac unit. While Liz lay in bed, the baby was monitored by machinery. 'Suddenly, an ominous bleep came from the machine. The baby was in distress.' An emergency caesarian followed and Liz woke, fearing the worst. Her husband reassured her. 'We've got a lovely little girl.' However, at less than 1lb 2ozs (500g), baby Annabel had only a 50 per cent chance of survival. Born at 28 weeks, she was so small that Mike's wedding ring slipped easily over her arm. She was rushed to the special premature baby unit at Poole Hospital in Dorset where she gained weight and was eventually allowed home. Sadly, Liz can't contemplate any further pregnancies because of her heart condition. 'But having her has made a complete difference to our lives,' says Liz. 'Without immunotherapy we had had no hope at all of a baby.'

Professor Beard's trials with immunotherapy were the first in the UK. Now other centres are taking up the treatment, including Cambridge. Dr Lesley Regan, Senior Registrar and Research Associate at the Rosie Maternity Hospital, Cambridge, has achieved a success rate comparable with St Mary's by her work in 200 cases. Coping single-handedly, she says, 'The only commodity I'm short on is *time!*'

She has been particularly successful with women patients who, as one patient explained, find her, '– sympathetic and direct without talking down to you. She doesn't try to pretend that she has the magic answer, but warns you first of all that the work is largely experimental.'

Dr Regan was fascinated by the immunological mechanism in women. She says, 'It would not be surprising if all embryo's were recognized as foreign by the mother and rejected, like any other dissimilar graft.'

'The foetus is genetically a different person from its mother and carries individual genetic identifying markers. These are called HLA antigens, which wave like flags from most cells in the body.

'It is thought that in a normal pregnancy the mother's immune system recognizes that the baby's cells are carrying foreign markers and responds by producing a blocking factor to prevent natural rejection,' says Dr Regan.

Doctors are working on research to find out more about this mechanism – the protective blocking response. It is known that it is a factor present in the serum of the mother's blood, so it has been suggested that it is a 'blocking antibody'. They have to find out whether the mother is producing this antibody as an indicator that her immune system has recognized the pregnancy and responded appropriately to prevent its rejection.

Why do some women fail to produce this protective response?

Many suggestions have been made: that the foetus is immunologically immature; that the mother is immunologically incompetent during pregnancy; that the mother and baby remain entirely separate, or that the womb is a 'protected site'. All these theories seem to have been discarded in the light of modern knowledge and the most likely reason is the possibility that failure to form blocking antibody is because the husband and wife have too many HLA antigens in common.

Doctors noticed that a woman who

recurrently miscarried with one partner might not do so with another. However, Dr Regan emphasizes: 'We have moved on in three years since I first wrote about this for the Miscarriage Association newsletter. It now looks likely that local factors working within the womb play an important part in suppressing the rejection factor. Perhaps it has been too simplistic to hope that general circulating antibodies would be responsible. In three years we have begun to see things differently.'

Doctors have known for many years that the chances of a kidney or heart transplant succeeding greatly increase if the patient has been given a blood transfusion just before the transplant. Research in 1981 (Drs Taylor and Faulk[13]) suggested that miscarriage patients might benefit from a blood transfusion with the aim of stimulating mass production of suppressive antibody. They reported the successful pregnancy outcome of three women who were given white cells from pooled donor blood.

Each of these women was found to have developed antibodies which could be shown in the laboratory to be directed at their partner's HLA antigens. It was suggested that the production of these anti-paternal antibodies had allowed the woman to mount the appropriate immune response and they were able to go ahead with their pregnancies.

The technique basically used at the UK immunotherapy centres is to infuse a quantity of whole blood or white cell fractions obtained either from multiple donors or from the woman's own partner. The patient's blood is re-tested about four weeks after treatment to see whether antibody production has occurred.

'Some patients never produce detectable levels,' says Dr Regan. 'But they still go on to have successful pregnancies.' Treatment just before conception or during the first eight weeks of pregnancy is reckoned to have the best chance of success. Although the initial results are exciting and successful Dr Regan warns that there is no guarantee that it will prove to be the answer for all couples suffering from recurrent miscarriage and as yet we do not know whether the therapy will have any long-term side-effects on mother or baby.

All the immunotherapy patients at Cambridge are closely monitored throughout their pregnancies and they are compared with a control group of volunteers – women who are embarking on their first, second, third or fourth pregnancy but have not suffered the complication of recurrent miscarriage.

'It was the most important journey of my life. There we were battling down to Cambridge in an old crock of a car, with Sally the cat miaowing madly all the way! But we had to get to the hospital so that we had the chance of having a baby.'

HELEN had had three miscarriages when her doctor referred her for immunotherapy in Cambridge. It was a long journey from their home in Blackburn, in the north of England.

She had had a fertility problem and been put on Clomid to stimulate ovulation. At 32, she had given up her teaching job in the hope that she would be under less stress at home and could have a successful pregnancy. In fact, she became pregnant while still working her notice, but lost the pregnancy, making it a total of four miscarriages.

Helen and her husband were both delighted to be offered immunotherapy. 'We were warned that the treatment was experimental, but we were still excited to be offered some help. My own doctor was interested in the work at Cambridge and gave us his full support.

'The journey was pretty disastrous. I hadn't been able to find anyone to look after the cat so she had to come with us.

'The car was so old we were worried we wouldn't get there at all. But we made it and my husband gave a pint of blood in the morning. We spent a chilly afternoon walking round Cambridge until it was time to go back to the hospital for me to be injected with the serum made from Ian's blood.'

Helen found the injections quite painful. 'I don't think I'm unduly soft when it comes to injections but, boy, did it hurt! My arm swelled up around the injection area and was extremely painful. The doctor said this was normal and the swelling would last a week.'

A few weeks later, they returned to Cambridge for more blood samples. 'This time we borrowed a car! We couldn't cope with our old faithful any longer. We were advised that it would be good to get pregnant within two months.'

Sadly, in spite of working with the calendar and trying desperately to conceive, Helen took a long time to become pregnant again. When she succeeded there were further problems. 'I felt sure I was pregnant as I was very sick but I couldn't get a positive pregnancy test result. Eventually, a hospital scan was done and the doctor broke it to me very gently.

'He said, "I don't known how to tell you, but you have an ectopic pregnancy." (Ectopic pregnancy – see Chapter 5.) All the staff working with him seemed upset as well, as they knew how hard I had tried for a baby. This was completely unrelated to the immunotherapy treatment.' After it was taken away, Helen went back to work briefly and became pregnant again. 'I think it was because I was busy thinking of other things and didn't have time to brood about babies! I wasn't at home going insane with worry about it all.'

Bed rest was recommended and Helen took that advice seriously. 'There were a couple of scares – some bleeding – but the pregnancy settled down and continued with no problems, ending with the birth of Amy, a perfect healthy child!'

At Oxford's John Radcliffe Hospital, Consultant Gynaecologist Dr Christopher Redman plans further trials.

'The immunotherapy trials at St Mary's were impressive. My trials will take it just a stage further and be helpful to all the women who hope it will work for them.'

Dr Redman is inviting women who have had three or more miscarriages to ask their doctor to refer them to him if they wish to take part. The aim is to assess the effectiveness of immunotherapy and, as it is a clinical trial, the women will not know which group they have been selected for. They do of course run the risk that they could be selected for the placebo group – the 'dummy' control group who do not receive the real treatment.

No matter what the outcome, Professor Beard is pleased with his results.

He admits to being sceptical at first, but says now: 'We can't put our hands on our hearts and say that we know how it works. But it *does* work and we don't seem to do anyone any harm!'

Progesterone

'I had one miscarriage and was terrified of it happening again. So in my next pregnancy my doctor gave me progesterone by injection. I am sure I wouldn't have my healthy son now – if it hadn't been for that!' KAY has no doubts that the treatment helped her, but treatment with hormones has long been the subject of medical controversy.

Certain hormones are, of course, essential for maintaining a pregnancy. Progesterone and HCG (Human Chorionic Gonadotrophin) are both important in 'feeding' the foetus and for some years it seemed to help to give one or other of these if the pregnancy seemed to be failing.

Dr Katharina Dalton, whose Harley Street practice in London is the centre for many women on various kinds of hormone treatment – notably for premenstrual syndrome – is enthusiastic about injections of *natural* progesterone. This is not progestogen, the synthetic progesterone, which she dislikes.

Says Dr Dalton: 'There is one group of women who have severe pregnancy symptoms very early on in pregnancy: nausea, vomiting, lethargy, irritability

and headaches. Many of these patients have had recurrent miscarriages. The progesterone level should be raised until the placental output is enough to maintain the pregnancy.'

It is important, emphasizes Dr Dalton, to get in quickly! 'Ideally, the progesterone should be given as soon as the woman knows she is pregnant and before there is any loss of blood or threatened miscarriage. I've seen many cases where the pregnancy had gone on to full term after this treatment.'

Dr Dalton has described treating 24 women who were threatening to miscarry with progesterone,[14] of whom fifteen had markedly severe pregnancy symptoms of sickness and vomiting. Of these, ten (66 per cent) went on to normal deliveries of healthy babies, whereas in the group of nine who did not have pronounced pregnancy symptoms, only one (9 per cent) had normal delivery.

Progesterone has been used in patients with recurring miscarriages for more than thirty years but there have been conflicting reports on its efficiency. In the 1950s, Dr P. F. M. Bishop reported an 85 per cent success rate in women with two previous miscarriages.[15] But controlled trials carried out by Dr G. I. M. Swyer and Dr D. Daley in 1953[16] found no significant success.

'Progestogens, believed to be a true progesterone substitute, then became fashionable with doctors for the treatment of recurrent miscarriages but with the realization that progestogens produced masculination of the female foetus all treatment – with both progestogens and progesterone – was stopped,' says Dr Dalton.

She feels that the dose of progesterone given was far too small and that doctors do not differentiate sufficiently between patients with severe sickness symptoms and those without. She also feels that women should be questioned about these symptoms much more closely in antenatal clinics.

Dr Dalton says: 'I am happy to give natural progesterone without any risks of side-effects during pregnancy. I have used it successfully to save a pregnancy and prevent miscarriage and also in the treatment of toxaemia.

'We've also found that when mothers have been on progesterone in early pregnancy their children have much higher educational attainments and are much more intelligent!'

Progesterone is used where some women have had *in vitro* fertilization treatment – 'test-tube baby' treatment. It is now the subject of intensive trials in Canada with Professor Daye of Hamilton, Ontario.

Many doctors are doubtful about hormone treatment for inadequate progesterone production, which is also known as corpus luteum deficiency. Their worries are based on problems encountered some time ago. In the 1950s and 1960s, oestrogen (stilboestrol) was given as a treatment for miscarriages but some of the daughters of the patients who were treated developed rare cancers. It is hoped that the Canadian study will discover more about the real value of progesterone treatment, but this is a long-term trial and results may not be available for some time.

Treatments for physical abnormalities

If your womb is 'a funny shape' it is not the end of the world and may not put paid to your pregnancy hopes! Doctors have delivered perfectly normal babies from wombs which were very odd shapes indeed! But sometimes an odd shape means that the baby has not enough room to grow, as is often the case in a womb with a septum (see Figure 5(b) in Chapter 5). If this could

be the reason for miscarriage, an operation may be performed.

At the age of 34, JOANNA was offered surgery to correct a bi-cornate (two-horned) uterus (see Figure 5(e) in Chapter 5). Her surgical history was already impressive: several D and Cs, an ovarian section for the removal of cysts, plus two laparoscopies. They had all been part of her uphill struggle towards a successful pregnancy. After thirteen miscarriages, she was beginning to feel that it was obsessional. She was then lucky enough to be seen by a top London surgeon. 'I was a little nervous at the thought of this quite big operation, but he explained to me how it would be carried out and described similar operations he had done successfully.

'So I began to feel quite optimistic. After thirteen miscarriages and still without a baby, I saw this as my only chance of motherhood and I was determined to go through with it.' She was in hospital for eight days and wrote up her diary for the benefit of other women. 'It occurred to me that a woman offered this type of corrective surgery might be reluctant to accept, simply because she has never had an operation before and is frightened by the prospect.'

Joanna wrote up the details, including the admission routine of shave and enema. 'Neither as bad as anticipated and soon over with. I had lessons from the physiotherapist on how to cough after surgery. Most important. Then a visit from the professor, who was to operate, and the anaesthetist. After supper, the 'Nil by mouth' sign was hung on my bed.

Thursday: Operation day. Would have loved a cuppa!

Early bath, donned special gown, routine check that I had no false teeth or other loose bits! Wedding ring taped over.

I would have had a relaxing pre-med injection but there was no time as the surgeon was ahead of schedule and already waiting for me in theatre. In the preparation room the anaesthetic was administered through a needle inserted in my arm and a nurse held my hand and chatted to me until I fell asleep. When it was all over I came round briefly in the recovery room and when I woke next, I was in the ward. I slept most of that day and night.

Friday: Still sleepy but sitting up in a chair and walking with some assistance to the bathroom. The drip in my arm didn't bother me but it did restrict movement somewhat and I needed help to wash. I had an early visit from the professor who had assisted in the operation. He assured me that all had gone well and I had an overwhelming feeling of relief that at last it had been done. Desperate for a drink, I was eventually allowed a few sips of very weak Bovril, followed an hour later by tea and toast. When these had no adverse affects, the drip was removed.

Saturday: Feeling very cheerful, walking albeit slowly, all day and eating like a horse! Some discomfort, due to a distended tummy, but no pain at all, thanks to the medicine trolley.

Sunday: Plaster removed, exposing an incision about 7 ins (18cm) across, neatly stitched with just one thread running the entire length with a bead at each end. Eat your heart out, Mary Quant! It was below the hair line and half an inch (about 1cm) lower than my early scar so I knew eventually it wouldn't show. Was allowed a salt bath. Absolute bliss. Started gentle exercise with the physio.

Tuesday: Had the stitch removed in a quick and painless procedure. The bead was snipped off at the end and pulled through. It tickled! The relief was instant. Movement was much more comfortable without the pull of the stitch. Suddenly, I got a bit tearful as I was missing my husband. Apparently the blues are quite common at this stage.

Sent home the next day, Joanna soon realized that she was more weak than she had thought in the hospital. Her husband had to leave her a packed lunch when he went to work.

'I seemed to have no energy or strength. My tummy was still enormous and I could only wear loose-fitting clothes. At first, I allowed it to depress and frustrate me. Three weeks later I was still feeling sorry for myself and far too conscious of every little twinge and flutter from my womb. But then overnight I felt myself getting better. I managed to wear a tight waisted skirt to a party and I began to do light housework.'

She was advised to wait three months before trying again for a baby. 'I had some object left in the uterus. This is to keep it in shape while it heals but it was explained to me that it would re-absorb. I didn't have to have it removed.

'I know that in the event of a successful pregnancy I should have a Caesarean in the 38th week. This would be done to avoid any damage to the uterus and any risks to the baby usually present at normal birth.'

Each case is different. There are different methods of correcting uterine abnormalities. Joanna's operation is known as a Tomkins Vieroplasty.

'Would I go through it again? Yes, I would. The fear, discomfort and inconvenience of it were short-lived. It has given me new hope and confidence. Even if I remain childless, I shall always be extremely grateful for all that was done for me and for the skill and dedication of those surgeons.'

For Joanna, a child did not come straight away. She was to have further treatment after her 'op'; but she did get her longed-for baby in the end. At the age of 37 years 6 months, she gave birth to a healthy son. So for Joanna, her big 'op' was definitely worth the trouble!

The D and C operation

The D and C is the familiar 'scrape' which is often done after a miscarriage to make sure that the womb is completely cleared out and will not become infected, and that all the products of conception - foetus, amniotic sac and placenta - have gone.

It is done under a general anaesthetic, often in one day - the woman is in hospital as a day patient or for only one night. D and C stands for dilation and curettage (see Figure 7). The cervix (neck of the womb) is first of all carefully dilated until it is open enough to allow the curette through. The curette is a sharp, spoon-shaped instrument

Figure 7 The D and C operation

(a) Dilation of the cervix

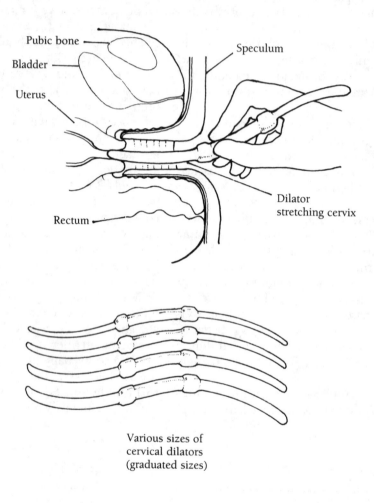

Various sizes of
cervical dilators
(graduated sizes)

(b) The curette

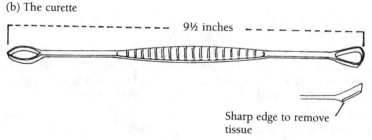

which is used to scrape the lining of the womb.

The womb (or uterus) is a hollow muscular organ shaped like a flattened pear. It has a lining which builds up due to hormonal influence from a permanent base layer of cells. This layer remains in spite of the periodic shedding of more superficial cells (menstruation).

At curettage, it is the superficial layer which is scraped away leaving the basement layer to provide replacement cells.

To widen the uterine cavity, dilators are used, each one fractionally larger than the preceding one and about eight steps are usually taken to open the cervix wide enough to accept the five millimetre-wide curette end. This is then drawn over the entire lining of the uterus and the superficial tissue is scraped off in strips.

The D and C is often done for reasons other than miscarriages. It may be used in infertility investigations, or to treat or diagnose heavy or irregular periods. After a miscarriage, it is not normally necessary to dilate the cervix as it is already open. Evacuation of a miscarriage follows a similar operative pattern to D and C. Doctors need to take great care as the soft pregnancy uterus is much more easily damaged than usual.

This is called E.R.P.C. – Evacuation of the Retained Products of Conception.

The D and C: What to expect afterwards

You will get some bleeding after the operation but it should not be more than a normal menstrual loss. If, after an E.R.P.C., the bleeding either increases or becomes offensive, you should contact your doctor. If the operation has not been totally effective, this could lead to haemorrhage or infection.

It is quite safe to take a bath afterwards. The next period is likely to arrive at about the same time and doctors advise that intercourse can be resumed after three days, though a D and C does not necessarily protect against further pregnancy, so contraception should be used.

The cervical stitch

If your cervix opens too soon so that the baby is lost, you have what the doctors call an incompetent cervix (neck of womb). This is caused by a weakness in the circular muscle at the neck of the womb which allows a premature membrane rupture (the waters break too soon), often after sixteen weeks of pregnancy.

This may have been caused by a difficult forceps delivery in the past or perhaps by over-enthusiastic dilation of the cervix in previous treatment.

If this is known about, a cervical stitch (or purse-string suture) can be inserted early in the next pregnancy – often at fourteen weeks – no sooner, as this might prevent an early miscarriage associated with developmental defects. The stitch is called a Macdonald or Shirodkar suture after the doctors who invented them.

After two miscarriages, NICOLA in Scotland had a cervical stitch inserted when she first became pregnant. Again, she was in hospital for five days for observation and rest after the general anaesthetic. At home, still under instruction to rest, she had some pink staining and again had to spend five days in hospital.

'Everything settled, but I continued to rest at home, although I did pop out for the odd grocery or two! My husband was very patient and did all the household chores. Anxiety was high for us both.

'The Shirodkar suture was removed during a normal vaginal examination when I had reached 37 weeks. Finally, at forty weeks, just 24 hours from my expected date of delivery, our son was born. Robbie was safely delivered, crying his little heart out! We also cried.'

Although Nicola had to take things easily, a cervical stitch should not normally interfere with daily routine. When it is in place, few women complain of any discomfort from it though the thread from a stitch can sometimes be felt by a man in intercourse. There may be a vaginal discharge. If this has an offensive smell, it should be reported to the doctor in case of infection. It is very important that the stitch is taken out before labour starts, so you should make sure that any doctor knows about it. The cervical stitch has a high success rate if it has been inserted early in the pregnancy.

The hysterosalpingogram

This is a diagnostic procedure in which a dye is inserted into the uterus so that any unusual shape, such as a bi-cornate uterus, will show up on X-ray.

It is a fairly uncomfortable procedure, in which the syringe is inserted into the vagina, and it can cause a period-type pain for a while. It is done in the first ten days of the cycle to ensure that the patient is not pregnant at the time.

The laparoscopy

Under general anaesthetic, often in hospital only as a day patient, the woman has a small incision made at her navel, which is invisible afterwards. A long thin 'telescope' type instrument is introduced into the abdominal cavity which separates the organs and gives the surgeon a good view of all the pelvic organs.

This way he can see exactly what is

going on. He can get a good idea of ovarian function, can see ovulation if it happens to be occurring at the time and check that the tubes are not blocked. As an aid to confirm that the tubes are clear he may well insert a dye. This is often used in cases of infertility.

Amniocentesis

Amniocentesis is a test to find out whether a foetus has Down's Syndrome or a neural tube defect such as spina bifida.

It is normally offered to all pregnant women over 38. It involves taking a small amount of amniotic fluid from the woman for testing, and is usually carried out at about sixteen weeks. The fluid is drawn through the mother's abdominal wall and the cells are grown in a culture medium to find out the chromosome make-up of the foetus. Amniocentesis may also be done at the request of the geneticist investigating a chromosomal problem.

There is a small chance of a miscarriage being triggered by this test. It is a very slight risk and a lot depends on the experience and skill of the technician carrying it out. The benefits of a 'clear' result can put your mind at rest for the remainder of the pregnancy! The worst thing about it is the long wait afterwards for the results to be ready. If they do spotlight a problem and you are expecting a handicapped child, you then have to make the dreadful decision about abortion.

A new kind of test – the chorion biopsy – involves taking tissue from the chorion, or placental membrane. This can be done earlier in pregnancy, but does carry a higher risk of miscarriage.

CHAPTER 15

When treatment succeeds

'Suddenly it was the happiest day of the year!'

'The doctors and nurses were rushing around. I could hear such panic in their voices. "Will this hospital take her? Will that one?" As I went unconscious I heard talk of an emergency Caesarean. Then suddenly the baby was here. A fine healthy boy! It was the happiest day of the year.'

When ROS wanted a baby it was quite a performance! She had such a series of difficulties and disappointments that her medical history reads like a book in itself. But Ros, former policewoman and former teacher, was plucky, single-minded and determined. She volunteered to inject herself in the abdomen twice a day for most of her pregnancy in order that a new treatment could be tried.

Using a one-and-a-half inch (38mm) syringe, she managed to give herself injections of the 'magic' drug. Her technical experience of administering the breathalyzer came in handy. 'The nurses had shown me how to inject myself and I could hardly trek backwards and forwards to the hospital every day.

'It was much more convenient to do it myself. I soon got used to it even if my stomach did end up looking like a black and blue pin cushion.

'At first, friends were horrified that I was sticking the needle into the area where the baby was but, after all, it was only a subcutaneous injection which means that it goes just below the skin. It wasn't going anywhere near the baby.'

The injections were suggested by Ros's consultant after she had suffered three miscarriages and was found to be 'rejecting' the foetus as 'foreign.' For medical reasons she was not eligible for the standard immunotherapy treatment (see Chapter 14), so injections of heparin, a blood anti-coagulant, were prescribed in the hope of saving a fourth pregnancy.

Ros's story had begun with the birth of her daughter, Sarah, her first child, with no problems. This was followed by three miscarriages and a cervical discharge problem which involved several D and C operations and a minor repair.

Ros remembers her surgeon's remark: 'We don't know what's causing the problem, but if I were you I would go away and get pregnant and perhaps flush it out.'

'I replied: "Yes, and risk losing a baby." In fact, I never dreamed that it would really happen but I did become pregnant shortly afterwards and at six weeks began to miscarry.'

This miscarriage was painless. She saw the nine-week-old foetus. 'It was lying in a bedpan, immaculately formed, its back in the classic curve. It looked like one of the pictures I had seen in the baby books I had studied so eagerly. The head tucked in, no neck to speak of. It really upset me to see it lying there in all that blood and mess. A nurse put her arm around me and just let me sob for about fifteen minutes. She was wonderful and I'm full of gratitude for her kindness, and for the care of all the staff.

'The consultant was good too. I was an impossible patient.

'Being an ex-teacher, I was armed with a list of questions. He just said, "Listen to what I have to explain first. Hear me out then you can ask what you like."

'Another of the doctors was very good too. He actually made a special appointment for me, outside his clinic hours, so that I could receive answers to my many queries. This was all done without my having to pay privately for the extra care.'

A further miscarriage followed. This time she was expecting twins. When miscarriage threatened, she was advised to rest. 'The worst four weeks of my life. I rested as best I could with a young child around, feeling I was a real handicap to the family. I once heard my young daughter tell her rag doll: "My mummy just sits and knits and cries." '

After the fourth week's rest a scan revealed that both of the twins had died in the womb. A third miscarriage was just as depressing. 'The baby had shrivelled and died very early on.'

After three miscarriages, a new doctor discovered that she was making antibodies to her husband and the injections of Heparin were introduced as soon as a further pregnancy was confirmed.

Ros's programme of self injections went well until at 25 weeks she had a haemorrhage and was again admitted to hospital in floods of tears. The bleeding was found to be coming from the placenta and the baby still seemed all right. But the bleeding started again the following week and she was rushed to the labour ward. 'This happened several times. Things would die down, then a panic when I bled again. I really didn't know whether I was coming or going! I was frequently in floods of tears over my husband and the nurses!'

At 31 weeks, crisis! Ros had a really severe haemorrhage and the hospital prepared for a Caesarean section. She had a six-pint blood transfusion and a close watch was kept all night. By morning, things had settled again.

'But my consultant felt that intensive care facilities were not too good at this hospital as they had lost a 32 and a 33 week pregnancy there the week before. He wanted me transferred to a hospital where intensive care would be better for the baby.' After the transfer and four hours in the new hospital, she haemorrhaged again and was rushed to theatre. 'As I went out I heard all the panic going on and I thought, "I hope that when I wake up it will all have been worth it." Everyone sounded so worried that I didn't think I would have a live baby.'

But she did! 'I woke up and Simon had been born. My husband had a Polaroid photo to show me. Apparently, the entire intensive care team had been there to help him breathe but he hadn't needed them. He was completely independent and breathing unaided. He weighed four pounds and six and a half ounces (2kg). He was an absolute little miracle with a strong pair of lungs!

'Suddenly it was the happiest day of the year. The happiest day ever! Not that I forget the babies I lost. I remember them in ordinary things. I can never throw out old flowers down the garden without thinking of them. I never stop grieving for them. Every time I see flowers on grass I think of the babies who might have been.

'Afterwards the staff at the hospital invited me to give them a talk on miscarriage from the patient's point of view. I am going to tell them, not to dish out the clichés. Someone said to me, "It's not fair, is it?" and those words helped me the most.'

CHAPTER 16

'Better luck next time . . .!'

You leave hospital after your miscarriage with the kindly-meant words ringing in your ears. The message that you can try again gives you a new boost of optimism. You will do as they suggest. 'Give it three months and try again.'

But when you have had one miscarriage, what are the chances of having another? Statistically speaking, after one miscarriage, there is a risk of just under 24 per cent of having another miscarriage. The risk rises to 26 per cent after two miscarriages and 32.2 per cent after three.[17]

But for the individual patient, the risk may be higher or lower depending upon specific circumstances and the cause of early pregnancy 'failures'. Doctors emphasize the importance of re-assuring patients that their prospects are not as gloomy as many of them think.

To help all would-be parents, Foresight is a British charity set up to promote care for parents before conception so that they have every chance of producing a healthy child. Founded by Mrs Belinda Barnes of Surrey, Foresight is backed by a team of distinguished medical advisers and has carried out extensive work in this area. It provides a wide range of literature so that would-be parents have the fullest information on health requirements before and during pregnancy. Some booklets also deal with medical research in detail for the benefit of the professionals.

Couples can be put in touch with their nearest doctor in private practice who runs a Foresight clinic. This is done several months before they hope to conceive so that they can have thorough examinations and tests, which include screening for any allergic syndromes or infections and hair analysis to show up any mineral deficiencies or the presence of toxic metals. Analysis of blood, urine or stools may also be involved.

The Foresight organisation sees the chances of 'better luck next time' as much greater than the statistics would imply.

'Tragically high figures only apply where no help is given,' says Mrs Belinda Barnes. 'If they set things to rights the outlook is much more encouraging. There will have been a reason *why* they miscarried. This reason is likely still to be present unless investigations have taken place. Setting things to rights includes insuring against deficiencies, cleansing heavy metals, sorting allergy, malabsorption, candida, rubella, toxoplasmosis and a whole range of genitourinary infections. It also includes helping the infertility associated with blocked tubes, polycystic ovaries, cervical erosion and such conditions as endometriosis.'

Foresight's record is impressive, with the number of miscarriages drastically reduced in couples who have been on the Foresight programme. For example, 100 couples with a history of miscarriages took part. They had had 182 miscarriages in all. The result was 110 healthy babies including several pairs of twins. Among them, there were three further miscarriages.

Also, 46 couples who had previously had 57 malformed or therapeutically terminated babies, after taking part in the programme, had 54 babies including one pair of twins. There were no malformations.

Advice on nutrition, health and testing for deficiencies and toxic metals, besides screening for infections, including rubella, candida, etc, – as previously listed – are all part of the programme. Although the Foresight clinics are privately run, involving a charge to the couples, some facets of this type of counselling before pregnancy are being made more widely available in the UK within the NHS.

In its booklet *Guidelines for Prospective Parents*[18] Foresight draws attention to the hazards surrounding us daily.

So, look to the future with a practical plan! Avoid, if you can, the following toxic metals:

Lead In spite of the new wave of enthusiasm for lead-free petrol, lead still comes mainly from traffic-exhaust fumes in the atmosphere. If you live in a heavy traffic area, net curtains near the windows may do something towards inhibiting lead's free entry into your house. Beware of lead in old paintwork too, and avoid stripping it as lead could be contained in the dust. Lead may also come via polluted water in old lead pipes – though since 1976 lead has been banned from use in water pipes. Many local authorities provide grants towards replacing lead pipes.

It is worth asking your water authority to check that the levels of toxic metals in your water comply with EEC and World Health Organization recommendations. A water filter is obviously a simple precaution, as drinking water is known to be contaminated with lead, aluminium, copper and sometimes mercury and cadmium. It also contains nitrates largely due to more intensive farming methods and the greater use of nitrogen fertilizers. Nitrites, a by-product of nitrates, have been shown to cause cancer in animals, though there is no evidence that they cause cancer in humans.

What harm does lead do? Lead can cause anaemia and nerve damage. It is also known to cause miscarriage, low birth weight or malformation and/or mental retardation.

Mercury High levels of mercury may come from tinned tuna fish or water contaminated by effluent.

In the garden Avoid weedkillers which may contain mercury.

On the farm Avoid seed wheat which may have been treated with mercury powder.

At the dentist Try to go to the dentist before you conceive. If pregnant, ask him to use a filling material which does not contain mercury, as some dental amalgams do.

What harm does mercury do? It has been associated with placental insufficiency and can cause miscarriage.

Aluminium Check your saucepans. If you cook vegetables in aluminium pans, some metal may come off in a layer on to the food. This is true with leafy green vegetables and some fruit.

Don't leave your tea to brew Don't 'stew' your tea, as a substance in tea-leaves will remove aluminium if it is left in the pot. Don't use an aluminium teapot at all.

Watch those foil plates and dishes! The familiar foil dishes we use to freeze food in may tend to give off metal into the food, especially where there is fatty pastry or acid in fruit.

What harm does aluminium do? It may have an adverse effect on the central nervous system. Aluminium has been linked with placental insufficiency and Alzheimer's disease, a form of premature senile dementia.

Copper The contraceptive pill is believed to cause copper levels to rise in the body. Copper also comes from drinking water in areas where the water is soft and acid.

What harm does copper do? It is known to cause premature birth in animals. High levels have also been linked with schizophrenia. Copper can also cause a zinc deficiency. Zinc is essential for the healthy growth of the foetus and a zinc deficiency has been associated with miscarriage.

Cadmium Too high cadmium is usually caused by smoking, or being in contact with other people who are smoking. It could also be linked with the plumbing, as some alloys in pipework can contain cadmium.

What harm does cadmium do? It has been linked with still-birth and low birth weight.

Avoid VDUs

If you have to sit at a Visual Display Unit for hours on end, you could put your pregnancy at risk. The evidence that VDUs could trigger miscarriage is inconclusive but it is sufficient to prompt the European Parliament to put out a directive on the use of VDUs, stipulating that employers should provide employment on alternative work for female VDU operators who become pregnant, without loss of earnings.

At Bush House, headquarters of the

BBC World Service, five out of fourteen VDU operators miscarried in 1988. These included secretaries and journalists who file their copy directly on to VDU.

The evidence against VDUs in relation to miscarriage has been mounting since 1979, when four out of seven pregnancies in the classified department of the *Toronto Star* newspaper in Canada resulted in babies being born with deformities.

Other evidence includes: *1985/6 University of Michigan, USA* – a slight but non-significant increase in miscarriages among women who used VDUs for more than twenty hours a week; *1986 Institute of Occupational Medicine in Poland* – an increase in miscarriages among women working at VDUs under high levels of stress; *1988 Kaiser Permamente, USA* – there was an increase in miscarriages among women working more than half the working week on a VDU during the first three months of pregnancy.

Many other incidents of miscarriage and birth abnormality clusters have prompted some trade unions to negotiate agreements stipulating that no woman who is pregnant should have to work at a VDU for longer than four hours at a stretch.

How do VDUs cause damage?

The most common type of VDU is the cathode-ray tube which produces ionizing radiation. It is known that ionizing radiation changes the structure of cells, producing conditions such as cancer, sterility, cataracts, birth defects and miscarriage. This can happen even when exposure is at a very low level.

Studies in the USA have revealed that some VDUs, particularly older models, leak ionizing radiation.

The controversy is over what level of radiation is harmful to our bodies. Most Western countries set their standards for exposure on the most common form of cathode-ray tube technology – the television set. But most people don't sit eighteen inches (45cm) away from their TV screen for seven or eight hours at a time as many VDU operators do in front of their screens.

One problem with VDUs is that the radiation is 'pulsed', giving off energy in short bursts. In animal studies, this pulsed radiation has caused foetal abnormalities. Insulating fluids used in VDUs (polychlorinated biphenols) are also suspected. Many women are confused about the risks they take.

ANNE, who is a translator, was trying for a baby and gave up travelling into the city every day to reduce stress. Instead she was working at home, spending long hours in front of her home VDU equipment.

'I started to wonder whether this was why I was miscarrying,' says Anne, who has had four miscarriages. 'There seemed no other reason. We don't smoke or drink and we are in the upper income bracket so it couldn't be a question of poor diet.'

Although the evidence against the VDU is inconclusive, in the USA trade unions and women's organizations have been campaigning for many years for legislation to protect VDU users generally and to give pregnant women, and those attempting to become pregnant, the right to transfer to alternative work.

In the UK, the VDU Workers' Rights Campaign has been campaigning for legislation along similar lines since November 1985.

Many influential trade unions in the UK have negotiated their own health and safety agreement on the subject. At the BBC in London, the National Union of Journalists took up the case on behalf of the women reporters who file their copy directly onto a VDU.

It was agreed that any request to be moved off VDU work from a woman who thought she was pregnant would not be 'unreasonably refused'.

If your work involves sitting for long periods in front of a VDU, make sure you get adequate breaks away from it and put the problem to your union representative or health and safety officer if you are not happy. In the present climate of opinion he is almost certain to listen!

Avoid illness!

If you can, that is! It is known that a high temperature can trigger a miscarriage and in pregnancy your immune system is less able to cope with the usual bugs in the atmosphere. It will probably be difficult to cope with all possible sources of infection but do your best. You don't have to plant kisses on the head of every little nephew with a runny nose!

In the same way make yourself scarce when you come across rubella (German measles). It is known that it causes blindness and deafness in babies and may also cause miscarriages. Mumps has also been under suspicion recently.

A previous abortion

Avoid morbid imaginings. If you have an elective abortion in your history you may be going through agonies of guilt because of it.

The truth is that it is extremely unlikely that a previous elective abortion (D and C) will have caused your miscarriage – that is, if it was done in hospital. The only exception is if it caused pelvic infection, which happens in hospitals occasionally and, more often, in back-street abortions. Pelvic infections can cause infertility. It has been calculated that it is twice as safe to have an abortion in the first twelve weeks of pregnancy than to go through with the pregnancy.

CHAPTER 17

Are you fit to have a baby?

'Surely there must be *something* we can do!'

'Can't the doctors prevent me from losing the baby?'

In the ominous days of threatened miscarriage, the days of slight bleeding and questioning: 'Is the baby all right?' 'Am I going to lose it?' 'What the hell is going on in my body?', it is a natural reaction to demand that medical science provides some solution.

As JUDITH admitted: 'When a miscarriage threatened I seemed to spend half my life in the loo, checking up that I wasn't bleeding. I got so worried that one day it took me half an hour to pluck up the courage to go into the bathroom!

'All the time I was thinking that the doctor would have some wonderful answer. He would stop the bleeding and save the baby! But when I saw him all he could suggest was bed rest!'

Sadly, no doctor can save a baby once the miscarriage has begun.

But there are constructive steps you can take towards giving your next pregnancy the best chance of success. Before you even start to try for a child you can change your life style to ensure that both you and your partner are in the very best – optimum – health for pregnancy.

Foresight, the Association for the Promotion of Pre-Conceptual Care, has studied the research of many workers in the field of nutrition, genito-urinary conditions, environmental hazard and foetal development. Foresight workers have spent the past ten years studying international research on reproductive health and have also looked at organizations concerned with the provision of organically grown food.

This experience, say workers, has shown them that adequate care before conception will help to prevent miscarriage and also prevent the birth of many abnormal, premature or small-for-dates babies.

Dr Roger Williams of Texas University has said in his book *Nutrition Against Disease*, 'If all human mothers could be fed as expertly as prospective animal mothers in the laboratory, most sterility, spontaneous abortions and premature births would disappear. The birth of deformed and mentally retarded babies would largely be a thing of the past.'[19]

Medical studies in the USA have

found that trace mineral deficiencies in diet can cause developmental failures in animals. At Wayne State University, for example, research showed that rats deficient in zinc, manganese and other trace minerals had reduced intelligence and poor mental development.

In its booklet, Foresight comments[20]: 'Many people wonder why in these days of so-called affluence, there should be such poor nutrition. We suggest that there are a large number of reasons: Modern food is processed, treated, pre-cooked, frozen, re-heated, tinned or filled with preser-vatives, chemicals or other additives to ensure long shelf life. All these pro-cesses destroy essential nutrients which were present in the food before processing.'

Two culprits get the blame for dietary deficiencies: fresh food which is often of low nutritional value thanks to fac-tory farming and artificial fertilizers, and convenience foods containing refined sugar and grains which have lost most of the vital B-complex vitamins and trace minerals needed by the body to metabolize carbohydrate.

These foods can 'steal' from the body's nutrient reserves, maintains Foresight, which also cites dangers in the 'common social poisons' of cigarette smoking, alcohol, the contraceptive pill and the 'coil' intra-uterine device. These, explain Foresight, deplete reserves of zinc, magnesium, mangan-ese and the B-complex vitamins A, C and E. Foresight's medical advisers for-mulate vitamin and mineral supple-ments specially for women, which can

be obtained from health food stores or by post. (See Useful Addresses p155.) As the organization is a non-profit-making charity, they try, they say, to keep prices low.

Pre-conception care is certainly becoming more of a priority with family doctors these days.

A doctor in general practice in the UK says: 'It is not enough these days to see a woman in the first twelve weeks of pregnancy. Any damage may have been done by then. To guard against miscar-riage and other problems, I want to see her and her partner the minute she even *thinks* about having a baby!'

While it is obviously important to be aware of hazards such as toxic metals and the importance of minerals and vitamins in the diet, it is also vital that a woman avoids worrying about it to the point of obsession and becoming stress-ed! In the same way that government advice on food poisoning can cause panic, so pre-conception advice could upset you if you don't keep a sense of proportion.

Take steps to get this kind of expert counselling if you possibly can. Clear the system of deficiencies. Prepare your body for pregnancy. However, don't go into a decline if you suddenly remember an odd occasion when you were in contact with, say, flaking lead paint. Just one occasion is unlikely to wreck your chances. So don't panic. If you are a paint stripper by profession and in contact with old lead paint every day, that is different. You could have cause to worry.

Even before you get to your pre-conception counsellor, you can make a start by making sure your diet includes plenty of the 'friendly minerals' – zinc, magnesium, calcium and iron – which go a long way towards counteracting the action of toxic metals, just as vitamin C can make up at least some of the lost vitamin if you smoke a cigarette. (Not that you would of course – knowing the disastrous effect that smoking has on pregnancy.)

How do you make sure your body is healthy enough to have a baby? How can you protect yourself against miscarriage?

Obviously you can't totally protect yourself. You can take all the precautions ever invented and *still* lose a baby. Sadly, that is life. However, the Foresight plan to get yourself fit before you start makes sense! And the first thing to consider is the length of time you wait before trying again.

LIZ said: 'I *had* to try again as soon as possible. In the end, the only thing that lifted my depression after a miscarriage was to find myself pregnant again.' Some doctors believe that three months is enough to establish a menstrual cycle and pinpoint when conception occurs. It need only take a few days for a full physical check-up of blood pressure, weight, blood sugar and any signs of infection.

Foresight says: 'Our advice is to wait as long as it takes to achieve optimum health with no deficiency in the system, no high levels of toxic metals, control of allergy and no genito-urinary infections. If these things are not given time and attention a woman may go right ahead and suffer a further miscarriage.'

It is important to leave a reasonable gap, as the latest research shows that following miscarriage or childbirth the chances of the next pregnancy miscarrying are higher when conception occurs immediately or shortly afterwards, although adequate pre-conception care can reduce these odds.

If you have a long standing condition such as diabetes, high blood pressure or epilepsy, it is advisable to see your doctor before getting pregnant. If you have a relative with a birth defect or chromosomal abnormality, genetic tests can provide reassurance. If a couple already has a Down's Syndrome child the odds of a second affected are increased from one in a thousand to one in eighty. Until recently, there was no evidence that pre-conceptional care could prevent a child being born with Down's Syndrome, but recent research on chromosomal abnormalities from the USA has suggested a link between low selenium levels and Down's Syndrome.[21] So the monitoring of selenium levels may possibly reduce these chances.

Consider your age

The chances of having a Down's Syndrome child increase with age. A woman in her early forties has a one-in-sixty chance of an affected child but in her middle forties the chance increases to one in twenty.

The selenium research, however, does give reason to hope that it is not a question of chance but is linked with a deficiency which can be investigated and hopefully, corrected.

Consider any infection

Any venereal infection in either partner should be cleared up before conceiving. Both partners need to be treated and checked again after treatment.

Consider the facts

In the UK, one in 44 babies are born malformed. In the USA the figure is even higher, being three times as many (UK, 2.27 per cent; USA, 6.8 per cent).

To protect yourself against the chances of a similar unhappy outcome, with a handicapped child, you should follow these guidelines:

1. Don't smoke or drink.
2. Eat sensibly.
3. Take daily exercise.
4. Check your blood pressure.
5. Avoid unprescribed drugs.
6. Clear up any vaginal infection, including thrush (candida).
7. Sort out allergies.
8. Avoid hazardous food additives.
9. Avoid pesticides.
10. Arrange for pre-conception care which includes screening for deficiencies.
11. Take care not to come in contact with German Measles. Better still, check your immunity and be immunized if necessary.

Adopt a healthy diet

Nutritionist Dr Barbara Pickard suggests[22]: Eat whole foods, including wholemeal bread and cereals; plus a range of animal foods, including liver, at least once a week (lamb's liver if you are worried about toxins). Plenty of fish, twice a week if possible.

'A pregnant woman should make up her own mind about eggs,' says Dr Pickard. 'Remember to buy them from the supplier you know and have used in the past and bear in mind that an egg is a wonderful "whole food" with nearly all the nutrients in it for a chick to grow. An egg contains a wide variety of vitamins and minerals and is an especially valuable food for pregnancy.'

Vegetarians

Vegetarians or vegans can easily substitute pulses, beans and nuts for the meat and fish. Dr Pickard suggests beans on toast, vegetables with rice and bean and vegetable soups. These are a good idea, she says, for meals which are not the main meals of the day.

Dr Pickard believes that a mixed diet is better for a pregnant woman than a vegetarian one. 'You miss so much in terms of zinc and iron when things like beef are cut out. It really is worth weighing up your priorities and working out whether for the sake of the baby, you can relax your vegetarian principles for nine months.' But there are mothers who do have successful pregnancies as vegetarians.

Vegetarians and vegans may be low on the important vitamin B12 which is contained in animal meats, liver, and to a lesser extent, eggs, brewers' yeast and dairy products. If you have been a vegetarian for three years or more, it is possible that you are deficient in B12, which can cause anaemia and exhaustion. It might be a good idea to supplement your diet with B12, but check with your doctor first.

Some experts suggest that a completely vegan diet should be abandoned while pregnant so that milk and eggs are included. Dr Pickard advises vegetarians to increase their intake of protein and high calorie products if they become thin in pregnancy. She also suggests energy-dense foods such as olives, chocolate, peanuts, coconut and vegetable oils. Eat fruit and vegetables from the following groups every day:

1 *Group rich in vitamin C* This includes citrus fruit such as oranges and grapefruit, strawberries and raspberries, tomatoes, watercress, green vegetables, potatoes.

Some experts warn against eating potatoes which have green patches, indicating a concentration of solanin which is poisonous. It is also a good idea to cook potatoes without peeling them or when peeled very thinly as the vitamin content lies just under the skin. Waterlogged, over-cooked potatoes have lost most of their vitamin content, as have any vegetables fried in reheated oil.

2 *Fruit and vegetables containing folate* (sometimes called folic acid) These include broccoli, brussels sprouts, oranges, pineapple and avocado, dates, nectarines and melon. Folate is needed for the development of red blood cells and the nervous system.

3 *All other fruits and vegetables* Cooked or raw, some of all these should be eaten every day. Vegetables can be substituted for fruit when fruit is very expensive. Some citrus fruit should be eaten every day.

At least a pint of whole milk (not skimmed) or yogurt should be consumed each day. Skimmed milk is not recommended since it was tried unsuccessfully for babies in Canada. For cheese, recommended varieties are farmhouse Cheddar or Cheshire.

A good mixed diet for normal pregnancy

There are several nutrients which are essential for healthy human pregnancy and which we may be neglecting. These are folate, Vitamin B6 and zinc.

Folate deficiency is suspected of being involved in neural tube defects (conditions such as spina bifida) and may also be linked with babies who have a low birth weight. Folate is also contained in liver, kidney, yeast, spinach and oranges. Vitamin B6 helps combat morning sickness in pregnancy and is contained in wholegrain products, liver, beef, oily fish, peas, beans, bananas, carrots, avocados, spinach and yeast. It is also contained in Brie and Camembert cheeses, but you may not wish to eat those because of the possible risk of listeria.

Zinc is essential in animal reproduction and is now believed to be important in human pregnancy. Women who do not eat enough zinc in pregnancy have an increased risk of a low-weight baby and there have also been suggestions that low zinc may be associated with congenital abnormality.

Zinc is contained in beef, seafood, oysters, liver, nuts, beans, wholemeal bread, cheese, carrots, sweetcorn, tomatoes, yeast, ginger and mustard.

Dr Pickard suggests a four food group scheme as an eating plan:

1 *Two helpings daily from group one: meat, fish, eggs and pulses.* Lamb, beef, pork, liver, kidney, chicken, herring, mackerel, sardines, tuna, white fish, eggs, nuts, peas, beans, lentils, seeds.

2 *Four to five helpings daily from group two: vegetables, fruit and juices.* Potatoes, carrots, swede, beetroot, parsnip, onion, leek, cauliflower, beans, cabbage, lettuce, watercress, spinach, broccoli, tomato, sprouts, oranges, apple, pear, banana, grapes, melon, grapefruit, soft fruit, dried fruit.

3 *Four to five helpings daily from group three: bread and cereals.* Wholemeal bread, porridge, muesli, Weetabix, Shredded Wheat, crispbread, brown rice, wholemeal pasta.

4 *Three to four helpings daily from group four: milk and milk products.* Milk, yogurt, cheese, cottage cheese.

Fresh food is obviously much better for us in many cases. Raw carrot, for instance, contains twice as much folic acid if eaten raw, than it does if it is boiled. Orange juice and/or orange will give plenty of folic acid and vitamin C. An orange 'drink' will give virtually nothing in nutrients.

Variety is extremely important. Beef is a good source of zinc but a relatively poor source of folate, whereas dark green vegetables give plenty of folate but are relatively poor sources of zinc.

Dr Pickard stresses that some traditional meals are well-balanced combinations: for instance, roast beef (meat group), Yorkshire pudding (cereal and milk group), potatoes and greens (vegetable group).

The traditional British cook has some virtues, apparently – and even the

Italians come in for praise. Their pizza has a bread base (cereal group), a small amount of fish or meat (meat group) with tomatoes (fruit and vegetable group) and a cheese topping (milk group).

How do you know if you are overweight for pregnancy?

The *Quetelet index* was introduced by a Belgian who weighed and measured vast numbers of people to come up with a useful guide to weight and height.

First weigh yourself in kilograms, then: (a) divide the figure by your height in metres; (b) divide the resulting figure by your height in metres again.

$$\text{Quetelet index:} \quad \frac{\text{weight in kg}}{\text{height in metres (2)}}$$

For example, if you are 5ft 4 inches (1.62m) tall and weigh 9st 3lbs (58.5kg) your Quetelet index is 22.3, i.e. 58.5kg divided by 1.62 twice. A Quetelet index of between 20 and 25 is fine for health and pregnancy. (See Conversion Table, Figure 8.)

If you find you are overweight – that is, you have a Quetelet index of more than 30 – you may run the risk of diabetes in pregnancy or high blood pressure. Eat three small but regular meals a day and concentrate on a balance from the four groups.

If you are underweight with an index below 20, mention this to your doctor and try to eat well during the pregnancy – otherwise you could have a smaller than average child.

Figure 8 Are you too fat to have a baby?

To work out your **Quetelet index** you will need to convert your height and weight into metric measurements.

$$\text{Quetelet index:} \quad \frac{\text{weight in kg}}{\text{height in metres (2)}}$$

Height (1 inch = 2.54cm or 0.0254m; 1ft = 0.305m)

ft.	in.	m	ft.	in.	m	ft.	in.	m
4	8	1.42	5	2	1.57	5	8	1.72
	9	1.45		3	1.60		9	1.75
	10	1.47		4	1.62		10	1.77
	11	1.50		5	1.65		11	1.80
5	0	1.52		6	1.67	6	0	1.83
	1	1.55		7	1.70		1	1.86

Weight (1lb = 0.454kg)

st.	lb.	kg	st.	lb.	kg	st.	lb.	kg
7	0	44.5	7	10	49.0	8	6	53.5
	1	44.9		11	49.4		7	54.0
	2	45.4		12	49.9		8	54.4
	3	45.8		13	50.4		9	54.9
	4	46.3	8	0	50.8		10	55.3
	5	46.7		1	51.3		11	55.8
	6	47.2		2	51.7		12	56.3
	7	47.6		3	52.2		13	56.7
	8	48.1		4	52.6	9	0	57.2
	9	48.5		5	53.1		1	57.6

st.	lb.	kg	st.	lb.	kg	st.	lb.	kg
9	2	58.1	10	3	64.9		4	71.7
	3	58.5		4	65.3		5	72.1
	4	59.0		5	65.8		6	72.6
	5	59.4		6	66.2		7	73.0
	6	59.9		7	66.7		8	73.5
	7	60.3		8	67.1		9	73.9
	8	60.8		9	67.6		10	74.4
	9	61.2		10	68.0		11	74.8
	10	61.7		11	68.5		12	75.3
	11	62.1		12	69.0		13	75.8
	12	62.6		13	69.4	12	0	76.2
	13	63.1	11	0	69.9		7	79.5
10	0	63.5		1	70.3	13	0	82.6
	1	64.0		2	70.8		7	85.8
	2	64.4		3	71.2	14	0	89.0

If you are overweight when you are trying to get pregnant:

1. *Don't* diet drastically, which could cause you to stop ovulating.
2. *Do* cut out all white bread, sugar, sweets, soft drinks, cakes, chocolate and biscuits.
3. *Don't* over-emphasize one type of food such as fish or meat and neglect things like potatoes, fruit and vegetables. Eating plenty of fibre-rich food is a good idea as you will feel full.
4. *Don't miss meals.* It only means you will make up for it later and overeat!
5. *Do* increase exercise gently, with some form of exercise two or three times a week – enough to make you out of breath. Half an hour's brisk walk a day is more sensible than rushing off to play squash, according to Dr Pickard, who also suggests turning down the central heating on the grounds that this will help your body to adapt to cold and keep it warm itself!

What can you do to treat yourself?

Many women feel that they can help themselves by treatment such as relaxation.

Professor Richard Beard emphasizes: 'Women must learn to relax so that the uterus does not contract and cause a miscarriage which can happen simply because of the mother's state of anxiety and tension.' Relaxation classes are obviously good.

A relaxation technique to practice at home

'When a woman has had a miscarriage she will probably be very tense in a further pregnancy,' says Polish-born midwife Mrs Olga Goodman, whose lessons in relaxation have calmed many mothers. She is a devotee of psychoprophylaxis, which basically trains women to breathe properly in labour. But she feels that it also helps a woman to cope with worry and stress in pregnancy.

'She should do this gentle exercise routine any time she feels stressed', says Mrs Goodman. 'The emphasis is on easy-going activity. There is no violent jerking or pulling of muscles which might upset the pregnancy.'

She suggests the following routine:

Lie down on the floor. Find a draught-free area and make yourself really comfortable with cushions under your head.

1 *Breathe in*. Place your palm or tips of your fingers in the arch of your rib cage just above your tummy muscles, which will find your diaphragm. Take a deep breath and expand your chest as much as possible. As you do this the diaphragm will go downwards as it flattens.

As you breathe in, lift your right foot and tighten it. Really feel it as you clench it, tightening up your toes and your calf muscle as you breathe in.

Then slowly breathe out through the mouth – as if you were cooling soup – very, very slowly, unclenching and relaxing your foot as you go.

And . . . relax. Flop.

Repeat this exercise with your other foot, always remembering to breathe out very slowly.

2 *Breathe in* (as before, feeling the effects on your diaphragm). This time clench your right fist and tighten your arm.

Breathe out slowly and relax.

Repeat this exercise with your left arm and fist.

3 *Breathe in*. This time tighten the chest muscles. Really feel the tension as you do it. Then slowly breathe out.

4 *Breathe in*. Now tighten the muscles of the pelvic floor – the ones you will use so much in labour! Breathe out slowly ('cool the soup') and relax. Let yourself really flop in-between each exercise.

5 *Breathe in*. Tighten the muscles of the face and scalp, pulling a screwed-up horrible face! Really feel it tighten. Then breathe out slowly.

And relax.

6 By now you should be feeling totally relaxed all over your body. Let yourself breathe quietly, feeling that every part of your body is relaxed.

'With this technique you should be able to control yourself when you drift into an anxious phase,' says Mrs Goodman. 'Do it as often as you feel the need, being sure that you are comfortable.

'Always use the floor as the bed is really too soft.'

'Most of my class end up asleep afterwards as it is so relaxing. It is also useful if you can't sleep at night. The whole routine takes no more than twenty minutes and can easily be fitted into the day.'

'Another plus point is that these breathing exercises are wonderful for labour – so you are not going to waste them!'

Can homoeopathy help you?

Some women feel that alternative medicine can help them.

KAY was suffering from anxiety in an early pregnancy which followed a miscarriage. 'I was worried all the time, convinced it would happen again. I also found that I was suffering terrible morning sickness.' She went to see a doctor of homoeopathic medicine. 'He gave me a pill – just one pill which I took a fortnight ago and the morning sickness had completely gone. I'm also much more relaxed.'

Says Enid Segall, General Secretary of the British Homoeopathic Association: 'It really does help in pregnancy to see a homoeopath.

'In fact, we recommend that a couple both seek help as soon as they decide they want a baby. The treatment ensures that both father and mother are in fine fettle before the birth. Then the treatment for the woman is worked out individually to keep her feeling well and relaxed.'

Homoeopaths claim that their treatments cope with many hazards of pregnancy: 'If the baby is lying the wrong way, one special treatment will even turn it round for you.' Homoeopathy can help prevent recurrent miscarriages. 'The treatment given', says Enid Segall, 'does not involve any drugs, so cannot harm the pregnancy.'

When you are fraught with worry in case you miscarry perhaps for a second or third time, it is tempting to turn to alternative medicine. Some women, like Kay, have been helped through pregnancy nausea, anxiety and tension by the elderly medical science of homoeopathy.

On the face of it, it sounds unlikely. Who would want to take remedies of sulphur, mercury, deadly nightshade (belladonna), poison ivy and anemone?

Those are some of the rather unusual ingredients contained in homoeopathic remedies, but their devotees say that they cannot possibly be harmful as they are administered in such minute amounts.

Homoeopathy has a large following in the USA. At its peak at the turn of the century one sixth of all US doctors and hospitals offered homoeopathic treatments. Its popularity declined due to the rise in modern pharmacology, but since the 1970s it has become popular again, as part of the new climate of interest in better diet, exercise and a respite from drug therapy.

But how can this system of medicine help a woman maintain her pregnancy? Phyllis Speight, who lives in a picturesque village in the English West Country, has been a lay practitioner of homoeopathy for over 35 years, and has written nine books on the subject. She says, 'Many women have come to see me suffering from difficult pregnancies.' One remedy she recommends is aconite.

Aconite (aconite napellus) is otherwise known by its traditional name of monk's-hood. Other suggestions for homoeopathic remedies which might help if a pregnancy is threatened include: pulsatilla (anemone) and belladonna (deadly nightshade).

'But it is very important that anyone wanting to try homoeopathic remedies, particularly in pregnancy, should consult a homoeopath and not try to treat herself,' says Phyllis Speight. We treat the whole person – not merely one symptom – and remedies have to be given after full assessment of the individual case.'

Homoeopaths believe that their remedies can be helpful in pre-conception care and in pregnancy for both mother and the expected child.

Homoeopathic remedies include the following:

Aconite is believed to act on the fear in pregnancy which in excitable women can cause inflammation of the uterus.

White oxide of arsenic (Arsenicum alba) is given to relieve intense anxiety in pregnancy and persistent vomiting.

Yellow jasmine (gelsemium) is recommended to prevent miscarriage from fright.

Kali carbonicum (otherwise known as potassium carbonate) may be suggested if you have a tendency to miscarry in the second month.

Quicksilver (the element, mercury) could be the answer if you have a tendency to miscarry in the third month, while the *anemone* (pulsatilla) could help if a miscarriage is threatening with recurrent bleeding.[23]

A slightly daunting list of remedies, especially in view of the modern information about the effects of toxic metals in pregnancy. But homoeopaths are anxious to point out that these remedies are so carefully 'potentized' and scaled down that you would actually be taking only a tiny amount and that it should be done only under the supervision of a qualified homoeopath.

As an example, the 6th centesimal potency is comparable to one drop of the substance (or mother tincture) diluted in the volume of fifty Olymic-style swimming pools!

How did homoeopathy begin?

Homoeopathy was launched in Leipzig by a German physician, Dr Samuel Hahnemann, in the early nineteenth century. It was first practised in America in 1828. Dr Hahnemann experimented with a technique based on 'the hare of the dog that bit you.'

He had studied the teaching of Hippocrates that 'like cures like'. While he was working on the translation of a paper on pharmacology he queried a passage on Cinchona, the Peruvian bark which is the source of quinine. He took a large dose of the cinchona and to his surprise found that he developed an attack of marsh fever. In those days 'bark' was a popular cure for marsh fever. He had found a drug causing symptoms that it was known to cure! Years of painstaking experiments – in which he 'proved' his remedies on himself and his family – followed, before his colleagues grew to respect his theories and stopped dismissing them as far fetched.

'Let like be treated by like' is the homoeopathic code. The term homoeopathy comes from the Greek word *homoios* meaning 'the same'.

How does homoeopathy work?

Suppose a cook is slicing onions and his eyes start to water and run, his nose is sneezing and watering – we'd consider that the pretty normal effect of the raw onion. But suppose we meet someone who has the same symptoms but is not slicing an onion – then obviously we would call that hay fever.

In that situation homoeopaths would offer an onion – allium sepa – as the remedy, but it would be a minute amount prepared according to exact homoeopathic instructions.

All homoeopathic medicines are very carefully diluted and shaken – 'potentised' – and practitioners believe that their remedies act on the body's defence mechanism, strengthening it and enabling the body to fight off the disease. Dr Hahnemann worked on the theory that by giving a homoeopathic medicine he was substituting a temporary drug disease for the natural illness. The defence mechanism would react to the drug by mobilizing its forces to expel it and simultaneously expel the natural disease.

Homoeopaths have a fascinating list of substances which they use as remedies, including herbs, flowers, plants, minerals, metals, even poisons. If you think that homoeopathy could help you, fine – but *do see a qualified homoeopath*. He needs to measure you up as a whole person and see the problem as it relates to you. You can't just rush out and help yourself to some yellow jasmine or deadly nightshade!

CHAPTER 18

The good news

'Charlotte Georgina came into the world on Monday at 10.33 a.m. weighing a healthy 7lb 6ozs [3.35kg], complete with dark brown curls and gorgeous blue eyes. She's an absolute peach!' Sometimes, even after several miscarriages and a lot of heartbreak, there is good news.

ALISON from Lincolnshire who desperately wanted a child (see Chapter 9) has at last been successful. Her fourth pregnancy ended with the birth of Charlotte Georgina and she wrote with the good news:

'She was born two days ago and I'm still quite emotional. The birth was an amazing experience. It hasn't sunk in yet that she is really mine.'

The cheering aspect of the Miscarriage Association's newsletter is that many women write with the good news – that they did have a baby in the end.

BABS, who has an infertility problem, found this irritated her.

'It used to upset me so much that other people wrote in to say they had succeeded in the end by getting pregnant immediately after a traumatic experience of miscarriage. My problem was getting pregnant at all!'

Most women feel that no matter how many pregnancies they have after miscarriage, they will still grieve for the one they lost. A new pregnancy does not replace the lost child.

Since the interviews for this book were done, many people have been in touch to bring us up to date with their news. At the time of going to press Kathryn Ladley is herself pregnant for the second time but continuing her work as secretary of the Miscarriage Association.

TRACEY who vowed she would 'jump over a cliff' if there was a baby for her on the other side has got her wish – a daughter Pippa Jay, who weighed 8lbs 3½ozs (3.73kg) when she was born after a sixteen and a half hour labour.

'It was such a long ordeal that in the end I had all the help known to woman,' says Tracey. 'Drugs, epidural, episiotomy . . . I must admit I was deeply grateful for all the help I could get!'

Tracey, who has a very slight frame, had had a cervical stitch from early in the pregnancy. She says Pippa is beautiful: 'Brown hair and blue eyes. Worth all the worry!'

SUSAN, the policewoman who 'sobbed in the scan room' has now had a daughter, Jessica, with no problems this time.

DENISE, who was told her baby was dead at 20 weeks, is now pregnant again, but rather nervous: 'It's difficult to relax after such an experience.'

JENNY, the secretary who found the silence from other people the hardest thing to cope with, has now had a son, James Matthew and says, 'He's a handful but I am totally happy.'

But Alison's letter is perhaps the happiest. She said, 'Charlotte looks a lot like her dad which is fine by him. Looking back it was all worth it. It hasn't by any means blocked out the past, but at least there was a reward at the end of it.

'To anyone who desperately wants a child and who has previously suffered a miscarriage . . . if they feel, as I did, that to be "complete" and "a real woman" the only way of achieving it is to have a child, then Charlotte has taken care of all that. I feel whole, completely at peace with myself. I no longer feel a failure and inadequate, as I did before. At last I can let out even more tears and a very big sigh, knowing that for me it is all over. I've made it.'

Glossary of terms used

In miscarriage you will hear many medical terms used. To save confusion, a rough guide to the words which will be tossed about!

Abortion The loss of a baby before it is able to live on its own. Doctors call all miscarriages 'spontaneous abortions'.

Amniocentesis Test of amniotic fluid taken from the womb to find out whether there is any possibility that it has spina bifida or Down's Syndrome.

Amniotic sac The 'bag of waters' which forms in pregnancy to protect the baby in the womb.

Blighted ovum An embryo which fails to develop at a very early stage of pregnancy. A blighted ovum always miscarries or is removed surgically.

Cervix Neck of the womb (uterus).

Chromosomes Genetic material contained in the nucleus of a cell, responsible for transmission of hereditary information.

Clomid Clomiphene. A pituitary stimulant which is prescribed to improve ovulation and promote the functioning of the corpus luteum.

Corpus luteum Small yellow body in the ovary which is responsible for producing progesterone.

Conception The union of an egg and a sperm to create a new life. Fertilization. The impregnation of the ovum by the spermatozoon.

D and C Dilation and Curettage. Expansion of the cervix and the scraping of the inner lining of the uterus.

Down's Syndrome (Mongolism) A congenital abnormality with facial and physical characteristics resembling the Mongolian race.

Ectopic pregnancy When a baby is implanted and grows outside the womb.

Embryo A fertilized ovum – or conceptus – of two to eight weeks' gestation.

Fallopian tube The tube that carries the ovum (egg) from the ovary to the womb. Named after the Italian anatomist Fallopius.

Fertilization The impregnation of an

ovum by the sperm to create new life.

Foetus The baby growing in the womb from nine weeks until birth.

Gamma globulin A protein substance in the blood which is important in the body's resistance to infection.

Gene Subsections of the chromosome responsible for carrying inherited traits.

Hormone A chemical produced in the blood. Hormones regulate reproduction and stimulate target organs such as the skin, the ovary, the womb.

Human chorionic gonadotrophin This hormone is produced in early pregnancy and seems to be important in maintaining the pregnancy. Sometimes given in certain types of infertility.

Human menopausal gonadotrophia A natural hormone use to treat infertility. Also known as *Perganol*. This is the drug which caused such 'fertility drug' furore over multiple births. But it rarely triggers multiple births these days as doctors have learned how to regulate the dose.

Hysterosalpingogram X-ray examination of the womb and Fallopian tubes.

Incompetent cervix Weakened cervix that is unable to stay closed in pregnancy.

Miscarriage Spontaneous loss of a foetus. Known medically as a 'spontaneous abortion'.

Neural tube defect Birth defect of the brain and/or spinal cord.

Ova Reproductive cells of a woman.

Ovary Female organs responsible for production of sex hormones and eggs (ova).

Ovulation Process by which a mature egg is produced.

Placenta The vascular organ which supplies the foetus with blood and nutrients (the 'afterbirth').

Progesterone A hormone important during pregnancy.

Rubella German measles. A viral disease which causes potential damage to the foetus.

Sperm Male sex cells: semen.

Threatened abortion Cramping pains and bleeding, opened cervix which may signal a potential miscarriage.

Translocation Abnormal rearrangement of genetic material during cell division.

Uterus Womb. The female organ of reproduction which contains the foetus.

Reference notes

1 Beard, R.W. (1987), *Recurrent Miscarriage*, a fact sheet for CHILD, the self-help organization for couples with infertility problems. Their address is 367 Wandsworth Road, London SW8 2JJ, UK. (Tel. 01-740 6605)

2 Robinson, H. (1975), The Diagnosis of Early Pregnancy Failure by Sonar, *British Journal of Obstetrics and Gynaecology*, 82: 849-57.

3 Jouppila, P. *et al.* (1980) Clinical and ultrasonic aspects in the diagnosis and follow-up of patients with early pregnancy failure, *Acta Obstetrica et Gynaecologica Scandivaca*, 59: 405-9

4 Pickard, B.M. (1984), *Eating Well for a Healthy Pregnancy*, Sheldon Press, London, UK

5 Huisjes, H.J. (1984) *Spontaneous Abortion*, Churchill Livingstone, Edinburgh, UK

6 Michel-Wolfromm, H. (1968) The psychological factor in spontaneous abortion, *Journal of Psychosomatic Research*, 12: 67-71

7 Corney, R.T. and Horton, F.T. (1974) Pathological grief following spontaneous abortion, *American Journal of Psychiatry*, 131: 825-7

8 Stack, J.A. (1980) Spontaneous abortion and grieving, *American Family Practitioner*, 21 (5): 99-102

9 Lindemann, E. (1944) Symptomology and management of acute grief, *American Journal of Psychiatry*, 101: 141-8

10 Huisjes, H.J. (1984) *op. cit.*

11 *Lancet* (1977) 'The abhorrence of still-birth', 4 June, 1188-90

12 *Lancet* (1983) Editorial: 'Maternal blocking antibodies, the foetal allocraft and recurrent abortion', 19 November, 1175-6

13 Taylor, C. and Faulk, W. Page (1981) Prevention of recurrent abortion with leucocyte transfusions, *Lancet*, 11 July, 68-9

14 Dalton, K. (1977) *The Premenstrual Syndrome and Progesterone Therapy*, Heinemann Medical Books, London, UK

15 Bishop, P.M.F., Richards, N.A. and Doll, R. (1956) *British Medical Journal*, 2: 130 Bishop, P.M.F., and Richards, N.A. (1952) 'Habitual Abortion – Further Observations on the Prophylactic Value of Pellet Implantations' *British Medical Journal* 1: 244

[16] Swyer, G.I.M. and Daley, D. (1953) 'Progesterone Implantation in Habitual Abortion' *British Medical Journal*, 1: 1073

[17] *Human Genetics* (1964) 'Spontaneous abortion risks in man: data from reproductive histories collected in a medical genetics unit', March, 16, 1: 1–23

[18] *Guidelines for Future Parents* (Revised edition, Nov. 1988) is published by Foresight, the Association for the Promotion of Pre-Conceptual Care, Godalming, Surrey, UK

[19] Williams, R. (1971) *Nutrition Against Disease*, Pitman, 1971, Bantam, 1973, London, UK

[20] See Note 18 above

[21] Gromadinska J., Wcasowicz W., Sklodowska M., Strozynski H. 'Glutathione peroxide activity, lipid peroxides and selenium status in blood in patients with Down's Syndrome' *Journal of Clinical Chemistry and Clinical Bio-Chemistry* May 1988 Vol. 26 (5): 255

[22] Pickard, B.M. (1983) Nutritional aspects of pre-conceptional care, *Midwife, Health Visitor and Community Nurse*, November

[23] Speight, P. (1985) *Homoeopathic Remedies for Women's Ailments* Health Science Press (C W Daniel Company Ltd, 1 Church Path, Saffron Walden, Essex, UK)

Useful addresses

The Miscarriage Association, P.O. Box 24, Ossett, West Yorkshire WF5 9XG, UK. Tel. 0924-830515.
For support and information after miscarriage (SAE). Self-help groups throughout the country.

AUSTRALIA: The Miscarriage Association already receives many letters from Australia and is anxious to set up groups in Australia. Contact UK Headquarters initially.

Family Planning Association of NSW Ltd, 161 Broadway, NSW 2007, Australia. Tel. (02) 211 0244.
This could be another helpful contact. The organization has offices in every state.

VDU Workers' Rights Campaign, City Centre, 32–35 Featherstone Street, London EC1, UK.

USA: The Pregnancy and Infant Loss Center, 1415E Wayzata Boulevard, Wayzata MN.55391, USA.
Non-profit making organization to sup-port families who are newly bereaved after miscarriages, still-birth or early infant death.

Resource Through Sharing, 1910 South Avenue, La Crosse, W.I. 54601, USA.

FOR BOOKS AND LEAFLETS ON PREGNANCY AND NUTRITION, contact Dr Barbara Pickard, Lane End Farm, Denton, Ilkley, West Yorkshire LS29 OHP, UK. (SAE)

Foresight. The Old Vicarage, Church lane, Witley, Nr Godalming, Surrey GU8 5PN, UK. Tel. 042879-4500. A wide range of booklets on pre-conception care including 'Guidelines for Future Parents', £2. Foresight Clinic Protocol. Please send SAE for leaflets. For postal service selling nutritional supplements including the Foresight range: Contact Mrs Aschwarden, Dellrose Cottage, Littlewick Road, Lower Knaphill, Woking, Surrey GU21 2JU, UK. Tel. 04867-88845.

Index